THE

STATE

OF

QUEBEC

Peter Desbarats

❧

THE
STATE
OF
QUEBEC

❧

A Journalist's View of
the Quiet Revolution

❧

McCLELLAND
AND STEWART
LIMITED
TORONTO/MONTREAL

To Marjorie,
for putting up with me,
and to Douglas,
for putting me up.

✻

Preface

This book was researched and written in a period of four months.

There were two reasons for haste. I am a working journalist employed by the *Montreal Star*, and while four months may seem a very short time in which to produce a book, it is a very long time to remain on leave of absence from a Canadian newspaper. I am grateful to my newspaper for this extraordinary opportunity. The second and more important reason is that the situation is changing so rapidly in Quebec, and there has been so little published on it recently in book form for English-language readers, that a longer period of research might have lessened the usefulness of the work.

My method of research, in addition to reading, was a series of more than seventy interviews, mainly with prominent Quebec citizens. All the interviews were on an off-the-record basis, which is why most of the quotes in the book are attributed to a type of person rather than an identified individual. This technique produced a sampling of unusually frank Quebec opinion. The time which important people devoted to these interviews, and the candour of their conversation, is evidence of Quebec's desire to have its ambitions and difficulties understood.

The full analysis of Quebec's quiet revolution remains to be made by sociologists, economists, historians, and other academic professionals. This is a "running report," written while the revolution is still in progress. True to my trade, I have refused to let this deter me from making a number of sweeping conclusions. If they provoke discussion within and outside of Quebec, so much the better.

PETER DESBARATS

Contents

❋

"What Montrealers know best about each other, they never say in public. Silence, an experienced and at times a cynical silence, has always been golden here."

HUGH MACLENNAN, 1959, IN HIS PREFACE TO *McGill — The Story of a University.*

"I have to say what I think."

RENÉ LÉVESQUE, QUEBEC'S MINISTER OF NATURAL RESOURCES, IN AN INTERVIEW WITH THE AUTHOR, JUNE, 1964.

Introduction

In the second half of its first century, Canada became one of the envied nations of the world. It was rich in natural resources, comparatively untroubled by racial or religious conflict, governed democratically through proven institutions, and sheltered by the double military might of Britain and the United States. Apparently an earthly paradise.

But within this young and robust nation was a stunted national soul or spirit or consciousness or whatever you wish to call it.

In the nineteenth century, it was bravely prophesied that the twentieth would belong to Canada. In 1964, Canadians are still waiting for the millenium. And the spirit of prophecy is, if anything, less confident. At times the future is regarded more apprehensively than hopefully.

Canada's current difficulty stems partly from the fact that it is a nation which has never been permitted to grow up. In the nineteenth century, even while the new Confederation was trying to loosen the strings that bound it to the British mother country, it was slipping inevitably and deeply into the lap of the United States. The history of Canada is largely a series of negative reactions to circumstances created by other countries. Transcontinental railways were built in Canada to counter American land-grabbers. It was a great day in 1939 when England declared war and Canada didn't, at least for a short time. In the Cuban crisis of 1962 Canada asserted its independence by refusing to fall in automatically with American defence preparations.

But an even more important reason for national immaturity is internal: Canada's failure to remedy a congenital and potentially fatal defect in its original composition. From the very beginning Canada has been not merely a confederation of former British colonies but an alliance of two distinct peoples, each with its own language and embryonic culture and its own distinct idea of national destiny.

Three possibilities have always existed for the "English" and "French" in Canada: assimilation of the French — an unspoken article of faith even today among many of the English, separation of the two groups into independent nations, and partnership. Up to the present the choice has been for partnership, but the terms of union have never been agreed upon finally by both parties. The nation has always been in a state of civilized civil war.

Like all wars, this one has had its ups and downs. Usually the crises were triggered in Quebec by events outside the province. In the nineteenth century the tragic Riel uprisings in Manitoba and Saskatchewan and the loss of the western provinces to the "English" sparked an upsurge of national feeling among the French in Quebec. More recently, two World Wars created a need for united national action by Canada and a consequent painful appraisal by French Canadians of the place of their own "nation" in the national effort.

After World War II, there were fifteen years of deceptive calm. Canadian politicians on both sides talked of the successful partnership of English and French and held up Canada as an example to less enlightened nations. But changes were taking place in Quebec, unobserved by most Canadians, which would lead to French Canada's first crisis of nationalism by spontaneous combustion. For the first time since the British conquest of 1760, Quebec was becoming truly North American. Prosperity was creating not only industrial development but a new type of French Canadian, educated, aggressive, and eager to play an active and complete rôle in his own time.

This was the beginning of what is now called "the quiet revolution" in Quebec — a revolution by French Canadians against the conservative Catholic ideals of a poor agricultural society and against dull acceptance of their position as a minority group rather than as an equal partner in Confederation.

More than a decade of ultra-conservative government in Quebec after World War II concealed this change but did little to deter it. When Premier Maurice Duplessis died in 1959 and his Union Nationale party began to crumble, all the pent-up forces of reform in Quebec burst into the open. The first to be surprised were the great majority of French Canadians who were themselves unaware of their own transformation. But soon after, the people of English Canada were jarred from their postwar complacency to face what appeared to be a serious threat to national unity emerging (rather tactlessly) on the eve of Canada's 1967 centenary.

This time it was not merely a repetition of familiar nationalist sentiment in Quebec. There were a number of disturbing new elements. As I mentioned above, the crisis was not provoked by anything in particular that English-speaking Canadians had done. It was generated inside Quebec by a popular feeling that at last French Canada's hour had arrived. It was nourished by an awareness among many French Canadians of the postwar struggle against colonialism in other parts of the world and a tendency for some French Canadians to identify themselves with other "oppressed" peoples striving to find their national identity. This introduced separatism into the Quebec scene as a legitimate if not widely accepted program of political action. Separatists who believed in the feasibility of turning Quebec into an independent French-speaking nation formed political parties and campaigned openly for support — a far cry from the days of the previous nationalist "wave" in 1937, when a French-Canadian priest was cut off the air for merely hinting at support for separatism in a radio broadcast.

On the extreme fringes of the separatist movement, small terrorist groups began to appear early in 1963. That spring, the terrorists planted a series of small dynamite bombs in mailboxes and against the outside walls of federal government buildings in Montreal. One man was killed and another seriously injured before the terrorist cell was broken by the police.

The arrest of most members of the original "Front de Libération Québecoise" failed to eliminate terrorism. Newspapers in Quebec continued to receive mimeographed bulletins from various "revolutionary armies" promising further violence. Early in 1964 there was a spectacular theft of arms from a federal military installation in Montreal and it was months before police rounded up all the missing weapons. On August 29, 1964, two men were killed when terrorists attempted unsuccessfully to raid a privately-owned arms store in downtown Montreal.

Separatists provided English Canada with another "shock treatment" in October, 1964, when Queen Elizabeth and Prince Philip visited Quebec City. For the first time in Canadian history, royal visitors to this country were given a cool reception. There were fewer spectators than military guards along most sections of the royal route through Quebec City and separatist demonstrators waged a sporadic twelve-hour battle with police on the first day of the Queen's visit.

This is the situation that faces Canada in the fall of 1964, and the outcome is far from clear. Already the crisis has produced a number of positive results. For several years now, Canadians have at least recognized it as a crisis. The official sign of this was the federal government's appointment of a large and expensive Royal Commission to study the whole question of bilingualism and biculturalism. There also has been an important decentralization of federal power, motivated largely by Quebec's desire for more fiscal and administrative autonomy within the federal structure.

English-speaking Canadians, on the whole, have made sincere efforts to inform themselves about developments in Quebec. The Toronto *Globe and Mail*, at the time of writing, has three full-time correspondents in the province. The *Toronto Daily Star* recently assigned its first full-time Quebec correspondent. Early in 1964 the Southam newspapers in English-speaking provinces began to publish a weekly column interpreting events in Quebec, and a full-time Southam correspondent in Quebec is likely. Many English-language newspapers now carry translations of editorials from Quebec newspapers. In the past few years there have been innumerable speeches, conferences, seminars, and television discussions in all provinces on the "French-Canadian problem."

At the same time, there has been a growing reaction in English-speaking Canada against "pressure" from Quebec. This, and not French-Canadian separatism alone, presents a real threat to Canadian unity. This is why it is urgently important to keep open the channels of communication between people of goodwill in both Canadas.

Of necessity, the job of explaining Quebec to English Canada falls to a large extent on English-speaking "Québecois." The French-Canadian writer is handicapped not only by language but by his isolation from English-speaking readers. At this time, particularly, he is usually so preoccupied with his own people, so inward-looking, that he has no time to write explanations for outsiders.

The English-speaking Quebecker has a foot in both camps. If he is of French-Canadian origin, like myself, he can understand and even share in the French Canadian's loyalty to his "nation within a nation." But he also has a vested interest in keeping Quebec within Confederation because only if there is a place for Quebec in Canada will there be a place for him in Quebec. This should be kept in mind in reading this book.

THE

STATE

OF

QUEBEC

1

La Belle Province

Only in Quebec would a young business executive talk fervently about "attachment to the land."

"I'm not thinking of farmers," he said right away. "It's a feeling that Quebeckers have. It doesn't exist in the other provinces. Or if it does, it isn't the same. What does it matter to a Torontonian if he lives in Ontario, Manitoba, or British Columbia? But this is the only place where I'm at home. It's more than a province."

The "État de Québec" is this: a state of mind. But it is also physical reality: land, water, people, universities, skyscrapers, and patates-frites wagons parked beside busy highways. There is no point in discussing the state of mind without first looking at the facts and figures.

There is an overpowering amount of land. Quebec contains 594,860 square miles of earth, rock, muskeg, and fresh water. This represents about 15 per cent of Canada's total area.

If one includes Labrador, as the separatists always do, the total rises to more than 706,000 square miles. Using this figure, separatists claim that an independent Quebec would rank fourteenth in size among the nations of the world and sixty-second in population. It would be a shade smaller than Mexico and contain a population about half that of Algeria.

It might be helpful to add that it would be about one-fifth the size of the United States and its population would be equal to about 2.8 per cent of the American population.

In size, at least, Quebec is second to none among Canadian provinces. The next largest is Ontario, with 412,582 square

1

miles of land and water occupying about 10 per cent of the national area. Quebec is more than two hundred times larger than Prince Edward Island, which also holds the title of province for reasons that made sense a hundred years ago.

Geography provides one clue to the French-Canadian tendency to regard Quebec as a nation within a nation. On the official Quebec map, which ignores the boundary drawn between Quebec and Newfoundland's Labrador by the British Privy Council in 1927, this nation-sized province is seen to be surrounded to a great extent by salt water — Hudson Bay and James Bay on the west, Hudson Strait and Ungava Bay on the north, the Atlantic Ocean on the east, and the Gulf of St Lawrence along part of its southern boundary. Only its southern and western extremities are plugged into a cup-shaped socket formed by Ontario and the United States. The map promotes the feeling that it would take only a slight tug to unplug the province from the rest of the country.

But much of this "Canadian Texas" might as well be on the moon as far as Quebeckers are concerned. The northern portion is a wasteland of tundra, rock, snow, and ice, valuable only for the hydro-electric potential in its distant rivers and the minerals embedded in its ancient hills. Settled for the most part along the banks of the St Lawrence River, Quebeckers have never felt the British Columbian's or Western Canadian's urge to possess their hinterland. Their "vision of the north," even by conservative standards, is regrettably weak. It has required elaborate colonization programs to drag them from settled areas.

Long ago the French Canadians dreamed of possessing a continent. When men could claim kingdoms in the New World with canoes, paddles, and glass beads, rosary and secular, French and French-Canadian explorers staked out a large part of North America, west to the Rockies and south to the Gulf of Mexico. Later, when possession depended on military power, people, and money, and the French Canadians had barely enough of these resources to ensure survival at home, the spirit of exploration withered. Only after World War II did railway lines, nourished by United States capital, creep above the fifty-first parallel to the mining settlements of Gagnon and Schefferville between five hundred and seven hundred miles northeast of Montreal. Except during Natural Resources Minister René Lévesque's holy crusade in 1963 to rescue the Eskimos of northern Quebec from the clutches of the federal government, where they had been dumped by a previous Quebec government, Quebeckers have paid little attention to their sub-Arctic regions. It has been English-Canadian painters, for the most part, who have seen poetry in the North and English-Canadian politicians who have tried to capture this poetry in political platforms.

For the average French Canadian, Quebec is the thin band of settlement that runs from the shores of the lower St Lawrence upriver through the centres of Quebec City and Montreal and along the north shore of the Ottawa River, with branches reaching into the Lake St John country north of Quebec City, the Eastern Townships southeast of Montreal, and the Abitibi region nestling against the Ontario border below James Bay.

Within this relatively small settled region there is more variety of landscape than is found in most countries. The Gaspé coast, spectacular on the rocky north shore of the peninsula, gentle on the south side, has a maritime tradition. On the north shore of the river and Gulf of St Lawrence, the mountains of the Canadian Shield cascade suddenly into the water, creating fjords of Scandinavian grandeur. Their rivers are bursting with power and their flanks are green with timber. Between Quebec City and Montreal the land rises more gradually from the river. Around Montreal the farmland is as flat as any western prairie. In the Eastern Townships the land has been cultivated for generations and the mountains are domesticated, skirted by apple orchards. There are Loyalist villages there that might have been plucked from central Ontario except that many of the shop signs on their high streets today are in French. Timber country runs north from Three Rivers and from the city of Hull, where mills pile up mountains of pulpwood in the shadow of the Parliament Building. Further north, in the Rouyn-Noranda region, the stacks of smelters tower over new cities that still look and smell raw.

The heart of the populated area lies between Quebec City

and Montreal. The metropolitan zones of Montreal, Three Rivers, and Quebec City contain almost half the population of the province — 2,550,000 people out of a total of 5,259,000.* These three centres are also the oldest urban areas in the province. Quebec City dates back to 1608, Three Rivers to 1634, and Montreal to 1642.

Because these dates appear to fade into antiquity in a confederation which is less than one hundred years old, many Canadians regard Quebec as an old region. This is not completely accurate. Settlement in Quebec did not follow the nineteenth-century pattern of Western Canada, where waves of immigrants washed over bald prairie, dispersed, seeped into the soil, and germinated farms and towns within a few years. French Canadians remained in the cities or on the strip farms along the banks of the St Lawrence and Richelieu rivers for a long time before significant numbers drifted into more distant areas. The settlement of the Gaspé peninsula by French Canadians in any real numbers occurred only in the nineteenth century. The Eastern Townships, now largely French Canadian, were settled originally by Loyalists trekking up from the south after the American Revolution. The Lake St John and Saguenay regions were populated extensively only in the nineteenth century. In the Abitibi region, members of today's middle-aged generation are the sons of men who cleared the land.

In 1760, at the time of the Conquest, about 65,000 French-speaking people faced 1,250,000 English-speaking people in North America. Cut off from French immigration, cheered on by a celibate clergy, French Canadians increased and multiplied after the Conquest at a rate rarely seen since the loaves and fishes. The population of Quebec today is more than 5,300,000 out of a total Canadian population of almost 19,000,-000 and a North American population of over 205,000,000.

For generations the birth rate in Quebec was a source of pride, if one were a French-Canadian politician, of concern,

* For the sake of easy reading, most figures are rounded off to the nearest thousand. As a rule, they are taken from the 1961 census. This is the first and last footnote to be found in this book.

if one were an Ontario politician, and of despair, if one were a French-Canadian mother. The hand that rocked the cradle never stopped. Even as recently as 1947 the rate of live births per thousand of population in Quebec was 31.1, considerably above the national rate of 28.9.

Long after the television set replaced the double bed as the focal point of married life in French Canada, the picture of huge Quebec families remained part of Canadian folklore. But by 1962 the birth rate in Quebec actually had dropped to 25.2 per thousand of population, almost the same as Ontario's, which had remained about static since World War II. In 1962, for the first time since the end of the war, Quebec's birth rate slipped below the national average.

Although this development might indicate that in matters of birth control not all Quebeckers are doing as the Romans do, or should do, it is a predictable trend in an increasingly urban and industrial society. With the exception of Ontario, Quebec today is the most "urbanized" of all the Canadian provinces. Almost four out of every five Quebeckers live in urban areas compared with a five-out-of-six ratio in Ontario.

The shift in Quebec has been sudden. Only fifty years ago, half the population of Quebec was rural.

While the birth rate was declining in Quebec, Ontario soaked up the lion's share of immigration after World War II. The peak was reached in 1957 when more than 282,000 immigrants arrived in Canada. Ontario received more than half of these while Quebec attracted only 55,000. Ontario offered to the immigrant a more prosperous economy and a unilingual society that did not press the immigrant into what often was, for him, a trilingual situation in Quebec.

Quebeckers themselves were uncertain about immigration. It was realized that Quebec required more people to keep abreast of Ontario but experience showed that most immigrants, for practical reasons, integrated with the small English-speaking group in Quebec. This was where the money was. A study of 230 immigrants in Montreal in 1958 revealed that 60 per cent regarded English as "the useful language" in Quebec while only 11 per cent preferred French. Even the small number of immigrants arriving in Canada from France

— only 2,674 in 1962 — found it difficult to integrate with the tightly knit community of French Canadians in Quebec.

The result was a great leap forward in Ontario's population and a much slower increase in Quebec's. In 1951 Quebec had 4,056,000 people compared with 4,596,000 in Ontario, a difference of slightly more than 500,000. By 1961 the gap had widened to almost a million people — 5,259,000 in Quebec against 6,236,000 in Ontario.

If the comparison between the two provinces is limited to Canadian-born population, the difference today is only about 600,000 people. Immigration has given Ontario the decisive edge. Unless there is an entirely unexpected return to the "revenge of the cradle" doctrine in Quebec, Ontario will be able to remain ahead in future on the basis of natural increase alone.

The only census age group in which Quebec has more people than Ontario is that between fifteen and nineteen years of age — those born during World War II. In this group Quebec has 467,426 people compared with 436,883 in Ontario. The current trend of natural increase in both provinces is shown in the figures for population in the zero-to-four age group — more than 740,000 in Ontario against 671,256 in Quebec.

A significant part of Ontario's population has been drawn from Quebec. Today there are more French-origin people in Ontario (647,000) than British-origin people in Quebec (567,-000). Quebec also supplied a good part of the original stock which has produced more than 232,000 French-origin people in New Brunswick.

Quebec's population is ethnically "purer" than that of any other province with the exception of Newfoundland and Prince Edward Island. More than 4,200,000 of its 5,259,000 people are of French origin. In Ontario, little more than half the population is of British origin, the other half being dominated by large groups of people of French, German, Italian, Dutch, Polish, Ukrainian, and other European origins. In the Prairie Provinces British-origin people form only one-third to one-half the total populations.

Although Quebec's population is unusually homogeneous, its non-French element is not as insignificant as many French

Canadians pretend. French-Canadian Quebeckers always tend
to exaggerate the British aspect of Ontario, where 40 per cent
of the people are of non-British origin, and neglect to consider
that more than 1,000,000 people in Quebec are of non-French
origin. They are aware of this alien element primarily in
terms of the financially dominant Anglo-Saxon group, but only about half of the non-French group in Quebec is of British
origin. There are 108,500 Quebeckers of Italian ancestry, 39,-
500 of German origin, 30,800 of Polish origin, 16,500 of Ukrainian origin, and 96,000 classified in the census as "other Eur-
oṗean." This "ethnic" group, despite the comparative slow-
ness of immigration into Quebec, is the fastest-growing segment of the Quebec population. It increased from 5.9 to 8.6
per cent of the total Quebec population between 1951 and
1961. In the same decade the proportion of British-origin population in the province decreased from 12.1 to 10.8 per cent
and the French-origin group slipped also, from 82 to 80.6 per
cent.

This being said, the fact remains that the people of Quebec
are to an unusual extent linked by a common ancestry. This
is the most unified and compact "national" group in Canada
today and the only one which exerts an important national
will which is sometimes distinct from the will of the larger,
newer, and less cohesive Canadian nation.

This ethnic unity in Quebec is reinforced by the domination of a single religion. About 88 per cent of the people of
Quebec adhere officially to Roman Catholicism. Compared
with the 4,636,000 Roman Catholics in Quebec, the province's
Anglican population of 194,000 and its United Church group
of 155,000 appear negligible. The fourth largest religious group
in Quebec is made up of 104,727 Jews, the second largest provincial Jewish group in Canada, only a shade smaller than
Ontario's 109,000-member Jewish community.

Although "Protestantism" is Ontario's dominant faith, Ro-
man Catholics represent the largest single denomination in
what French Canadians still regard as an "Orange" province.
There are 1,873,000 Roman Catholics in Ontario; the United
Church there has 1,641,000 adherents and there are 1,118,000
Anglicans.

Religion is a factor in keeping intermarriage between French and English in Quebec to a minimum. An examination of the 1951 census figures showed that only 15 per cent of the married Quebec women of British origin had French-Canadian husbands and only 18 per cent of the British-origin husbands had French-Canadian wives. In Ontario, on the other hand, more than one-third of the French-origin people have married outside their ethnic group.

More one-sided in ethnic and religious composition than most other provinces, in language Quebec is more diverse. About three out of five Quebeckers speak only French, but in Ontario five out of six people speak only English. This English-only proportion is even higher in all other provinces with the exception of New Brunswick. Almost half of all Canadians who speak both French and English are French-Canadian Quebeckers, although they represent less than one-quarter of the national population. The fact that 4,270,000 Quebeckers gave French as their mother tongue in the 1961 census but that only 3,254,000 Quebeckers speak French alone indicates that, very roughly, about 1,000,000 of Canada's 2,231,000 French-English bilinguals are French Canadians living in Quebec. The obvious explanations for this are the dominance of English in North America and its position as the main executive language in business in Quebec.

Despite the relatively heavy invasion of the second language, compared with other provinces, French remains in a strong enough position in Quebec to be used as a normal language of government, popular culture, and retail business. Its position as a living "national" language is far from precarious. There is in Quebec today a solid block of over three million unilingual French-speaking Quebeckers supplied with newspapers, magazines, theatre, radio, and television in their own language. The survival of this unilingual core after more than two centuries of virtual isolation from the parent culture argues against the disappearance of the French language in Quebec in the predictable future.

The same thing cannot be said about the survival of French outside Quebec. There are today almost one million Canadians in the other provinces whose mother tongue is French.

But experience has shown, apart from the case of New Brunswick, that their assimilation is almost inevitable. Contributing to this trend are intermarriage, difficulties involved in supporting French-language schools without government assistance, and the absence in many areas of French-language radio, television, and daily newspapers.

This book is primarily about Quebec and is not the place for a full discussion of the problems faced by French-language minorities in other provinces. But it can be noted in passing that their reaction to the changes in Quebec is ambivalent. On the one hand, they are proud of the advances being made by Quebec. Every increase in Quebec's prestige bolsters their pride in their own heritage. But they rightly regard extreme nationalism and separatism in Quebec as a threat because these doctrines imply the abandonment of any attempt to promote bilingualism and biculturalism in all provinces.

It is already evident, from the preceding pages, that when Quebec looks at English Canada, it looks primarily at Ontario. Not so many years ago, in Quebec, comparisons between the two provinces were made in terms of "apples and oranges." The economic superiority of Ontario was placed beside an alleged cultural and "spiritual" superiority in Quebec. Even within Quebec, the situation of French and English was treated in the same incompatible terms. In the words of a French-Canadian writer, "the French Canadians came to believe that they would remain inferior economically but that they were already superior in religion, fine arts, ways of life and human values."

Only in recent years has a significant number of influential French Canadians wondered seriously if their magnificent "way of life" could endure on shaky economic underpinnings. This sense of doubt has led to an honest look at their economic position, particularly with regard to Ontario. The results of this comparison have been bitter medicine for a proud people. It is all too evident that Quebec was — and is today — a second-rate province in economic terms.

Personal income in Quebec in 1962 was $7.6 billion compared with $12.2 billion in Ontario. Personal income per capita in Quebec in 1962 was $1,417. It was $1,939 in Ontario.

Much of the difference in incomes is explained by the relatively depressed state of agriculture in Quebec. Only 10 per cent of the total land area of Quebec is arable and barely half of this is actually farmed. Experts in the province's Department of Agriculture have estimated that Quebec is self sufficient only in dairy products, blueberries, and farm forestry products. Almost one-quarter of the farming operations in Quebec, including more than 10,000 full-time farm enterprises, are classified officially as failing to produce enough income to enable a man to live (under $250 a year). Only 40 per cent of the farms in Quebec produce revenues exceeding $2,500 a year. Average revenue from the sale of farm produce per farm in Quebec in 1962 was only $4,569 compared with $7,337 in Ontario.

Although the disparity in incomes in the two provinces is not quite so glaring in other fields, it is still significant. Wage earners with elementary-school education in Quebec earn an average of $2,805 a year, about $400 less than the comparable wage in Ontario. Quebec wage earners with university education earn an average of $5,776 a year compared with $6,170 for their opposite numbers in Ontario.

The Ontario work force contains a much higher proportion of skilled and educated professionals. There are 19,676 male professional engineers in Ontario compared with only 12,463 in Quebec. The census category of "male physical scientists" is almost twice as large in Ontario as in Quebec. There are 1,117 male architects in Ontario, only 894 in Quebec. There are almost ten thousand draughtsmen in Ontario, barely more than five thousand in Quebec. Ontario has more than 17,000 science and engineering technicians; Quebec has only 11,780.

In commercial occupations, the differences are even more striking. There are 10,432 male sales managers in Ontario, only 5,364 in Quebec. Ontario has more than 1,200 male advertising managers. Quebec has less than 450.

The one hopeful comparison: Quebec has approximately as many teachers as Ontario.

Ontario's higher income structure contributes to a much

higher level of business activity. Quebec's population is approximately 83 per cent of Ontario's, in terms of numbers, but retail sales in Quebec amount to only about two-thirds of the Ontario figure. Quebec has 29.9 per cent of all the stores in Canada, but these account for only 25.5 per cent of national retail sales. Ontario has 34.1 per cent of all the stores in the country, and they account for 38.6 per cent of all sales.

There are almost twice as many home freezers in Ontario as in Quebec and almost twice as many automobiles. The median value of dwellings in Quebec is $10,004 compared with $12,952 in Ontario. Ontario has more than twice as many single dwellings. Average monthly cash rent in Quebec is $59. It is $76 in Ontario. Federal statistics classify 194,343 Ontario dwellings as "crowded." Almost 260,000 Quebec dwellings are in the same category.

Enough statistics. More than enough from Quebec's point of view.

As a general rule it can be stated that living standards improve west of Quebec and deteriorate as one moves east. But favourable comparison with the Maritime Provinces is cold comfort for Quebec. As one of the two senior partners and founders of Confederation, as the homeland of a distinct national group which always has considered itself to be one of the two original blocs of Confederation, Quebec takes as its natural standard the largest and most powerful English-speaking province. To tell a Quebecker that he is more prosperous than a Newfoundlander is akin to asking a Calgarian to compare his standard of living with a Baffin Islander's.

There is more to the Quebec-Ontario comparison than traditional rivalry. French Canadians now realize that Quebec's second-rate economic position affects their whole position in Confederation. It produces feelings of resentment and inferiority in Quebec and affects the prestige of the province in other regions.

As a civil servant in Quebec City said, "Who ever bothered to learn German until Germany became a powerful nation?"

The disparity between Quebec and Ontario convinces most French Canadians that not only has English Canada failed to live up to the "spirit" of Confederation but that Confederation has helped to lift Ontario into a dominant economic position.

In his book *La Libération Économique du Québec*, Professor Raymond Barbeau of the University of Montreal's commerce faculty gives the separatist interpretation: "It is undeniable that Ottawa and all the Anglo-Saxon banking and financial institutions of Canada substantially assist Ontario to dominate the Canadian economy. . . . The standard of living for Ontario people is higher than it is in the rest of Canada because Confederation has granted privileges to them, and always grants privileges to them."

This is one separatist assumption that is shared by many French Canadians. A prominent French-Canadian politician in Ottawa said, "As long as the standard of living in French Canada is lower than it is in Ontario, French Canadians will blame the rest of Canada for their economic situation."

Is this fair?

The question is almost beside the point. It cannot be answered simply and conclusively. Extremely to the point is the fact that the "dollar gap" between Quebec and Ontario is one of the first things that a French Canadian sees today when he looks at his own province and the rest of Canada. It must be narrowed if Quebec is to become a self-confident partner in Confederation; and the rest of Canada, in its own interests, should support efforts which the Quebec government makes to narrow it.

2

Montreal

In the nineteenth century, Lord Durham at one point wanted to make Montreal the capital of a new province containing the Eastern Townships and the eastern part of Upper Canada, separating Upper and Lower Canada. The city exists today as a distinct entity within the province.

In some respects, it sets the pace for Quebec. In others, it no more represents a microcosm of French Canada than does Toronto. Because Montreal makes more noise than the rest of the province put together, through its powerful newspapers, both French and English, its radio and television stations, its bubbling artistic and academic life, the image that Quebec transmits beyond its borders is primarily a Montreal image. Often it is a distortion of the true picture.

But there is no doubt at all about the city's importance as a centre of population and economic activity.

With a population of more than 2,000,000 people, Greater Montreal is the largest metropolitan area in Canada. It contains three-quarters of Quebec's urban population. About two out of five Quebeckers live in metropolitan Montreal, while only two out of every six Ontario residents live in Toronto.

Apart from the "frontier" region of the north shore of the St Lawrence River downstream from Quebec City, which contains less than 2 per cent of the province's population, Montreal is the fastest-growing region in Quebec. In the decade ending in 1962 its population increased by 43 per cent. Quebec City's population increased by only 20 per cent in the same period.

With about 40 per cent of the total Quebec population, metropolitan Montreal contains more than 50 per cent of the province's purchasing power. Fifty-three per cent of the annual retail sales in Quebec are made in this region.

The metropolis contains 41 per cent of the province's manufacturing industries. They employ 55 per cent of Quebec's manufacturing labour force and the value of their annual shipments amounts to 55 per cent of the provincial total. In the economic sphere and within the limits of Quebec, Montreal occupies a far more dominant position than does Paris in France, the city that is often cited as the model of the octopus-metropolis. Using an apt and absolutely untranslatable word, a French writer has described Montreal as being more "tentaculaire" than Paris.

Part of the reason for this is the absence in Quebec of medium-sized cities. There is a vast difference between Quebec and Ontario in the numbers of people living in cities of from 30,000 to 100,000 population — 934,000 in Ontario against only 384,000 in Quebec. Quebec has no Hamilton, although there are plans to create a steel centre between Quebec City and Montreal; no Oshawa, although General Motors has announced that it will build an automobile plant on the northern rim of the Montreal metropolitan area; and on the whole, relatively few small cities outside the Montreal region which act as secondary points of economic activity.

From its earliest days, Montreal benefited from its strategic position athwart the St Lawrence River at its junctions with the Ottawa and Richelieu rivers. The Ottawa gave the city an early importance in the fur trade; the Richelieu provided a line of communication with the United States; and the St Lawrence co-operated by degenerating at Montreal from a deep-sea highway into impassible rapids. The city's harbour, a thousand miles from the open sea, became one of the continent's greatest ocean ports.

Montreal's earliest rival was Quebec City, thirty-four years older and a centre of both business and government administration in the days of New France. But as long ago as 1753, the old capital was beginning to appear effete beside its bustling competitor. In that year a writer remarked that the inhabitants of Montreal "are much more lively, active, bold, enterprising and warlike than those of Quebec City."

Shortly after the Conquest it was evident that Quebec City was out of the running as a commercial rival, although not as a centre of intellectual and political influence nor as the nursery where the most beautiful women in French Canada are cultivated. But in the following century Toronto began to blossom on the shores of Lake Ontario. In recent years it has almost surpassed Montreal in population, become the home of the most important stock exchange in the country, and developed as a rival pole of attraction for the head offices of national corporations.

In the past decade Montreal might easily have started an accelerating slide toward genteel poverty. There were many who speculated that it was about to play the Edinburgh of central Canada to Toronto's Glasgow. But the city had maintained sufficient economic vitality to benefit from the same buoyant conditions that were affecting Toronto. In the fifties and sixties, both national railways, with head offices in Montreal, embarked on major building programs. Dorchester Boulevard became a new "skyscraper row" flanked by the towering head offices of Hydro-Québec, Canadian Industries Limited, the Royal Bank of Canada, and the Canadian Imperial Bank of Commerce.

At the same time, Quebec's quiet revolution electrified the general atmosphere in the province and its metropolis. There is no way to measure the transfer of energy from French-Canadian nationalism to economic activity, but there is some relation between the heady political climate in Quebec in the sixties and the noticeable quickening in other areas of human interest. One obvious result was increased government spending on roads, bridges, the Montreal subway, schools, and such ambitious cultural projects as the Place des Arts concert hall and the 1967 World's Fair.

Good trends in the North American economy were another factor. It is a bit frightening to speculate about what might have occurred politically in Quebec in the early sixties if unemployment had increased sharply and government at all levels had found itself in a tight financial bind.

The concentration of economic activity in Montreal is due also to the fact that virtually all English-speaking Quebec capitalists live and work there.

Montreal is the only city in North America, Quebec the only province or state, where the majority population, descended from the original European stock and speaking one language, is dominated economically by a minority of relative "newcomers" speaking another language. In this respect, Montreal may be unique among the major cities of the world's developed countries.

The "English" population of Quebec is numerically small. Less than 600,000 people, or 10.8 per cent of the province's 5,259,000 people, are of British origin. Almost 700,000 Quebeckers give English as their mother tongue. The actual English-speaking group, containing as it does most of the immigrant population, is somewhat larger.

The English in Quebec are concentrated in metropolitan Montreal. Of the 700,000-odd Quebeckers who have English as their mother tongue, more than 436,000 live on Montreal Island and the adjacent Ile Jésus. If the region on the south shore of the St Lawrence River opposite Montreal Island is included, almost three out of four English-speaking Quebeckers live in the Montreal metropolitan area.

Outside of Montreal, English-speaking people show the same tendency to concentrate in urban areas. The largest single group is in Hull, across the Ottawa River from the national capital, where 20,841 people give English as their mother tongue. There are 14,243 mother-tongue English in Quebec City and 11,344 in Sherbrooke. A comparatively high proportion of English-speaking people is still found in the Eastern Townships, where they were once the dominant group. But in no rural census division in Quebec do English-speaking people form the majority today with the exception of Pontiac in the northwest corner of the province.

The mother-tongue English element in Quebec represents only 13 per cent of the total population. But on the Island of Montreal it accounts for almost one-quarter of the population. In some municipalities on the island, the English vastly outnumber the French.

Montreal's English-speaking population includes virtually all members of what one might call the "Anglostocracy" of the province. This is the financial élite that dominates English-speaking Quebec, French Canada, and, to a lesser extent, Canada.

The word "dominates" has to be understood, of course, in the Canadian context. In Quebec, as in Canada, many of the most important financial interests are non-Canadian.

In a speech made in March, 1964, to an American audience, Professor Donald Armstrong, director of McGill University's School of Commerce, stated that American companies control 45 per cent of all manufacturing, 60 per cent of petroleum and natural gas production, and 52 per cent of mining and smelting in Canada.

"Moreover the control by United States companies of Canadian industry is increasing," he said, "and it is the rising trend as much as the present weight of the American presence in Canada which is troubling some Canadians."

The same situation prevails within Quebec, except that English-speaking Canadians control most of the small segment of pie left over after the Americans have helped themselves. And the English-Canadian presence in Quebec is far more evident than is the American presence in the rest of Canada. The Anglostocracy tends to stick out like a sore, if well-nourished, thumb. It attracts most of the fire of French Canadians concerned about the lack of French-Canadian economic control in Quebec.

A French-Canadian member of the federal cabinet said, "The average French Canadian knows only that all the owners are English. He doesn't make any distinction between English Canadians and English-speaking outsiders. It all adds up to economic inferiority."

The English-speaking element in Quebec lives in virtual isolation. It long ago gave up significant official participation in the municipal politics of Montreal and plays only a minor rôle in provincial politics. It is divided from the majority French-Canadian group by religion as well as language.

Children in Quebec learn to accept this division as a normal condition of life from the moment they start school. Quebec is the only province with two distinct and equal public school systems. The religious division extends from the beginning of elementary school to the end of secondary education. Roman Catholic children go to Catholic schools and all others attend Protestant schools. School taxes are paid according to the denomination of the taxpayer.

Unofficially, there is a third system for English-language Catholic children. This comes under the predominantly French-language Catholic system, much to the annoyance of many English-speaking Catholics who feel that their interests are often neglected. There have been demands from English-speaking Catholics from time to time for their own school system.

There are also a small number of French-language Protestant schools in the Montreal area operated as part of the Protestant public school system.

There is little meaningful contact and co-operation between English and French in Quebec. As far as bilingualism and biculturalism are concerned, the great experiment in Quebec, after more than two hundred years of shoulder-to-shoulder existence between English and French, is a flop. Pierre Chauveau, the first premier of Quebec, said in 1876 that "in social and literary terms, we are far more foreign to each other than the English and French in Europe." The late Stephen Leacock contemplated Montreal from the windows of McGill University, grinned, and said:

> *Each race sees too well the faults, too dimly the merits, of the other. The English think that many of the French are priest-ridden; the French think that many of the English are badly in need of a priest. The English think that those of the French who are crooked are crooked in a selfish, petty way, using favoritism for little jobs. The French think that the English, when crooked, are crooked in a big unselfish way, stealing a million at a time out of franchise and giving silver cups to golf clubs.*
>
> *Merit, we say, passes unrecognized. All the English admit that, but for the French, Montreal would have had prohibition. But they differ in their degree of gratitude.*

Dr W. E. Lambert of the Department of Psychology at McGill University wrote in 1960 that Montreal is a "community whose history centers largely in a French-English schism which is perhaps as socially significant for the residents of the province of Quebec as that between the North and South is for Southerners in the United States."

This division can be regarded from two angles. If contact and co-operation between the two races is expected, the Quebec picture is bleak. If merely existing side by side without open warfare is regarded as an achievement, the French and English have, in a negative way and to a minimum extent, lived up to the official "Concordia Salus" (Our Salvation is in Concord) motto of the City of Montreal. This is the kindly interpretation given by Hugh MacLennan in a 1959 preface to a small historical work on McGill University.

For two centuries [he wrote] the city has been compelled to live schizophrenically in order to live at all. Two races, or at least two languages, share the living space on Montreal island, and they were once bitter enemies. On many of the grounds which produce murder, the two basic linguistic groups of the city are still opposed, yet it is a fact that they do not dislike each other (except sometimes theoretically), and that in the last two centuries they have never seriously offered violence to one another. Tact and compromise, a remarkable talent for sensing the motive of another person, all this combined with an amused tolerance of public scandal, have made this harmony possible. What Montrealers know best about each other they never say in public. Silence, an experienced and at times a cynical silence, has always been golden here.

In the short space of five years since Hugh MacLennan wrote this, violence has been offered, seriously enough to kill three Montrealers and mark another for life. The sense of tact and compromise noted by Mr MacLennan has suffered a setback. The golden veil of silence is in tatters. For the past three years in Montreal, all the "unmentionable" aspects of French-English relations have become subjects of everyday conversation, ad nauseam.

The same has been true, to a lesser extent, in other parts of Canada. But nowhere has the Great Debate raged as fiercely as it has in Montreal, for Montreal is the national laboratory of bilingualism and biculturalism where the two language groups are compressed by circumstances into an explosive mixture. The failure of the English-French partnership in Montreal is at the root of the problem in Quebec and Canada.

3

❧

The English Chez Nous

Every French Canadian could write the obituary of a typical member of the Anglostocracy of Quebec:

Born of wealthy parents of English or Scottish origin on the upper slopes of Westmount, he attended private schools before entering McGill University, where he frittered away his undergraduate years in fraternity houses and at the Ritz; afterward he toured the Old Country prior to assuming his rightful place behind his father's roll-top desk on St James Street, where he devoted the rest of his life to screwing the French Canadians.

Like most caricatures, this one has a germ of truth. As one can still find "habitants" in Quebec who look as if they were born in the woodcarving section of the Canadian Handicrafts Guild, one can also locate specimens of Anglostocracy in Montreal who fit the traditional picture down to the last syllable of drawled bastard British. But they are rare birds.

There is, of course, an Anglostocracy. There are good reasons for believing that there always will be. But the Anglostocracy has undergone striking changes in the past century. It is probably accurate to say that a majority of its members no longer possesses the three cardinal virtues of British origin, Protestant religion, and Montreal ancestry.

The Anglostocracy in Montreal dates back to the second half of the eighteenth century, to the years immediately following the British Conquest in 1760. One would like to recall a Mayflower and a band of hardy pioneers but unfortunately they do not exist. There was instead what General Murray, surveying his army's group of English-speaking camp-followers after the Conquest, described as "the most immoral collection of men I ever knew."

His reports contain further descriptions of this original group of sturdy Englishmen:

All have their fortunes to make, and I fear few are solicitous about the means where the end can be obtained. . . . Little calculated to make the new subjects enamoured with our laws, religion and customs, far less adapted to enforce these laws and to govern. . . . Magistrates were to be made and juries to be composed from four hundred and fifty contemptible sutlers and traders.

From this group of old contemptibles, reinforced by immigration, sprang a class of sutlers and traders of no mean proportions which not only dominated the province economically but threatened for a time to snow under its prolific French-Canadian population by sheer weight of numbers. It is a fact little known outside of Quebec, rarely forgotten in the upper echelons of the Anglostocracy, that English-speaking people once formed the majority in Montreal and made a valiant attempt to grab the rest of the province for themselves.

Reinforced by Scottish, Irish, and Loyalist settlers, the English-speaking element in Quebec grew from almost zero in 1760 to 215,000 people by 1851, according to the statistics presented in 1959 by Professor Raoul Blanchard in his comprehensive work, *Le Canada Français*. They formed 54 per cent of the population of Montreal and more than a third of the population of Quebec City. But even more surprising is the fact that by 1851 there were 170,000 English-speaking people scattered throughout rural Quebec. The English mother-tongue population of Quebec today, beyond the limits of metropolitan Montreal, Quebec City, Three Rivers, and Hull, is no larger.

If the total of 215,000 Quebeckers of British origin in 1851 is accurate, and if it is compared with 567,000 Quebeckers of British origin listed in the 1961 census, it means that this segment of the Quebec population has increased by only 2.5 times in the past 110 years. In the same period, the total population of the province has increased by almost six times. The British-origin element in Quebec declined in relative numerical importance because of a lower birth rate, emigration, and, in some cases, assimilation so total that English names assumed French spellings and even the memory of British ancestry was lost.

Midway in the last century English-speaking people dominated both shores of the Ottawa River, the Eastern Townships, and a chain of settlements in the Laurentians north of Montreal. The first Roman Catholic parish in the Laurentians was founded by the Irish in 1832. Even today Laurentian place names such as St Calixte de Kilkenny recall an Irish colony swamped by a later wave of French-Canadian settlement.

Irish immigration enabled Montreal's Anglostocracy in the mid-nineteenth century to command a numerical majority in the city. The Irish population of Montreal increased from 7,000 in 1830 to 13,300 in 1861, when it was more than 20 per cent of the city's entire population. These were approximately the years of English-speaking majorities before French-Canadian fertility and immigration into Montreal from rural Quebec began to swing the balance back toward its original position.

Great fortunes were made by some of the early English-speaking arrivals. The claim that French Canadians and British Canadians in those days had equal business opportunities is ridiculous. Cut off from French sources of capital, ruined by inflated paper money in the final years of the French régime, living under an alien government and dependent on British shipping, French-Canadian merchants were behind the eight-ball from the time of the Conquest. Some idea of the capital resources of the newcomers can be gained from a contemporary report that one Boston businessman, Thomas Walker, arrived in Montreal shortly after the Conquest with 10,000 pounds sterling. A survey of the harbour of Montreal in 1866 showed that 96 per cent of the ships in port were British.

Yet there are still many Montreal businessmen who are convinced that French-Canadian and British merchants started out on an equal footing after 1760 and that the Englishmen's success was due to some mysterious inherent talent.

"The French Canadians had the same opportunities but they simply weren't interested in business," said the president of one of Canada's largest corporations.

"The ones who did go into business were individualists and preferred small businesses.

"The average Anglo-Saxon, on the other hand, is commercially-minded. It's a racial characteristic. He's concerned with earning a living. His life's effort is commercial."

It is certainly true that many of the early Anglostocracy arrived here with nothing but ambition. But the whole psychological climate was encouraging for them, discouraging for the French Canadians. For the new arrival, the Conquest represented a chance to enter a rich new territory. It was a beginning. For the French Canadian, 1760 was the end — a sort of death that he is only now starting to forget. French-Canadian historians such as Michel Brunet of the University of Montreal are absolutely correct when they say, writing from the depths of their own intuitive knowledge of the French-Canadian group, that "one must never lose sight of the fact that a foreign conquest and occupation is the greatest impact a society can ever meet."

"As a collectivity," Professor Brunet has written, "the Canadiens were doomed to an anemic survival. One must never forget that to survive is not to live."

From the beginning, many of the important English-speaking families tended to be rather exclusive, and not only with regard to the French Canadians. Stephen Leacock, describing the American occupation of Montreal in the winter of 1775-76, wrote that "in social life, the 'best' people kept away from the Americans." Leacock also cited the privately printed history of "one of the best-known families of Montreal" to illustrate the rarity of marriage between English and French. Less than a dozen of the five hundred names in the genealogy could be identified definitely as French.

One of the early exceptions to this rule was James McGill, who married the widow and simultaneously acquired the four children of Joseph Amable Trottier Desrivières. The experiment was a happy one for James McGill, as far as we know, but not for the university he founded. After McGill's death in 1813 it required more than twenty years of legal wrangling to dislodge his wife's nephew, Francis Desrivières, from the property now occupied by McGill University. The struggle between the Royal Institution for the Advancement of Learning and McGill's French-Canadian nephew has been described by Hugh MacLennan as "fascinatingly squalid."

The nineteenth and early twentieth centuries were the salad days of the Anglostocracy in Montreal. Even after the English-speaking people slipped into a numerical minority, they kept a firm grip on the reins of financial power. There were fabulous financiers such as Sir Herbert Holt, president of the Royal Bank of Canada and twenty-six other major business enterprises, director of about three hundred companies. His Montreal Light, Heat and Power Consolidated was the largest privately owned utility in the world before it was expropriated by the Quebec government in 1944 for $112 million. In his book *Flame of Power*, Peter Newman quotes a Montreal lament of the late 1920's: "We get up in the morning and switch on one of Holt's lights, cook breakfast on Holt's gas, smoke one of Holt's cigarettes, read the morning news printed on Holt's paper, ride to work on one of Holt's streetcars, sit in an office heated by Holt's coal, and then at night go to a film in one of Holt's theatres."

These were the days when proud Anglocrat names such as Morgan, Allan, Hickson, Van Horne, and Strathcona were inscribed in the history of Montreal and above the portals of many of its leading commercial and educational buildings. And it was a time when the lives of many of the city's leading Anglo-Saxon capitalists confirmed the suspicion in French-Canadian minds that profit-making was somehow tied up with Protestantism. It did not seem at all strange seventy-odd years ago for a prominent Montreal banker like George Hague to follow up the success of his book *Banking and Commerce* with another volume entitled *Some Practical Studies in the History and Biography of the Old Testament*.

Writing in 1942, Leacock recalled a colleague at McGill University talking about the "oppressive and plutocratic" atmosphere generated by this élite group in Montreal in the early years of this century. Leacock himself pinned down a typical specimen:

Those of us who remember the era can think of one such, richest of all perhaps, whose simple evenings were spent alone, reading the evening newspaper under a droplight, smokeless, for he knew too much about it, drinkless, for he didn't care for it, and speechless, for he seldom had much to say, except "yes" for another million.

"Forty years ago," recalled a veteran of St James Street over lunch in the Montreal Club, "three main groups controlled everything in Quebec. Webster, Holt, and Montgomery. You couldn't do a thing without their co-operation."

He chuckled to himself, "The manœuvres they pulled would land them in jail today.

"They were exclusive all right, but not just toward the French Canadians. It was hard enough for an English-speaking person to break in. The exclusiveness of the English-speaking businessman today stems directly from the feudal system established by those old cliques."

Only the very rich or astute could wend their way confidently through the web of family, financial, religious, political, and even regimental ties which bound together the Anglostocracy. In the Montreal Stock Exchange, members still tell a story which originated in the days when the Exchange contained a potent Black Watch clique. As a joke, this clique blackballed an applicant for a seat on the Exchange because he was an officer in a rival regiment. The applicant committed suicide.

"Today I don't think that I could name the six most important business figures in Montreal," mused the St James Street veteran over his coffee and cigar. "The money is spread out more. And the leading men are quieter. You never hear of them. People like ———, the president of ———. You never hear of him and yet he's one of the big Canadians.

"His father sold pharmaceuticals. He himself didn't even go to college.

"There's another man I do business with, an immigrant. When he came here less than twenty-five years ago, he had very little. I guess that he's made about $100 million since then.

"Yes, things are changing. I'm a director of about thirty companies and every one has a French Canadian on the board. Often the same French Canadian, admittedly. It's hard to find the right men. We always advise a new American firm coming in here to get a French Canadian on the board. 'Yes,' they say, 'but where can we find a good one who'll see eye-to-eye with us?' There aren't many, that's true. There won't be, as long as the school system and the church system is as it is. But we've got to find them.

"Of course, the majority of my friends don't agree with me," he explained. "They're old-line Canadians who can't change their ideas."

What ideas?

"Oh, they talk about encroachment by the French Canadians. But they don't know why. To be quite frank, they don't really think about it much."

He looked about the spacious dining-room of the club.

"We're not as exclusive as we used to be," he said. "We've got quite a few French-Canadian members. There's the French-Canadian table over in the corner."

Viewed from the outside by French Canadians, the Anglostocracy looks as solid as Westmount Mountain. In reality it is a system of distinct worlds, separated sometimes by distances that could be described in terms of light years if there were much illumination moving between the worlds, which there is not.

The Jewish world in Montreal stands so far apart that it will be described in a separate section. There is a fairly large English-speaking middle class which rarely mixes socially with the Anglostocracy or, for that matter, with the English-speaking peasantry of the poorer districts. If he has an ear for dialect, the middle-class English-speaking resident of Notre Dame de Grace has little trouble distinguishing between Summit Circle English and Verdun English, the former with its clipped, pseudo-British accents and the latter with its trace of Irish sing-song and its prevailin' tendency to forget the "g" in "ing" endings.

There is the English-speaking Catholic world which holds itself aloof in education and, to a certain extent, in social life from the Protestant Anglostocracy. It has its own "establishment." When Eric Kierans was named Minister of Revenue in the Quebec government, non-Quebeckers assumed that the ex-president of the Montreal and Canadian Stock Exchanges would speak for the Anglostocracy in the provincial cabinet. But every Montrealer knew that Mr Kierans was one of the city's "Irish." Despite his business background and academic record as a former director of McGill University's School of Commerce, he was not a fully qualified member of the Anglostocracy. It was known that he had attempted, without success, to place a Jew in a seat on the Montreal Stock Exchange and had even gone so far as to support changes in voting regulations on the Exchange to weaken the stranglehold on membership exerted by older members of the Anglostocracy. Worse than that, he had lectured in French at the University of Montreal while he was president of the Exchange.

Mr Kierans confirmed the Anglostocracy's darkest suspicions when his first political speeches seemed to indicate that he had "gone over to the other side."

Some months after he was sworn into office, during a meeting with members of the Anglostocracy, the president of a large corporation said to him, "Look, Eric, you're getting to be one of the crowd. You're a Catholic and all you want to do is throw out the dirty Protestants."

The manager of a French-Canadian businessmen's organization confided, "Mr Kierans is a special case. He understands the French-Canadian mentality. I only wish he understood the English as well."

English-speaking Montrealers promote a deceptive appearance of unity by segregating themselves physically from the French Canadians in Montreal. The traditional line of division, along St Lawrence Boulevard, with the English to the west and the French to the east, is still roughly accurate. Montrealers raised in Westmount or Notre Dame de Grace frequently know less about the opposite end of their city than well-informed tourists.

Municipalities with English-speaking majorities are concentrated on the western portion of the Island of Montreal. Statistics of the 1961 census, which fail to list such small and almost purely English municipalities as Hampstead and Montreal West, give Côte St Luc the highest ratio of English to French — nine to one. The west-end lakeshore suburbs are next — eight to one in Beaconsfield and six to one in Pointe Claire. In Westmount and the Town of Mount Royal, Westmount's "little brother" linked to downtown Montreal by the tunnel under Mount Royal, the ratio is about three to one.

In the City of Montreal itself the English mother-tongue group is outnumbered about four to one.

The geographic separation of French and English is reflected in the formal social life of the city. Each group has its own clubs, such as the St Denis Club for the French, the Mount Royal and St James Clubs for the English, and the Montefiore Club for the Jews. Golf clubs reflect the same divisions to some extent.

While there is no clear-cut discrimination against French-Canadian members in English clubs, as there is in some against Jewish members, their French-Canadian membership actually is low. According to comments from both sides, there appear to be more English members of French clubs than vice versa. In at least some of the French-Canadian clubs there is a rule of thumb that the English-speaking membership should not exceed 25 per cent of the total. English-speaking Montrealers who want to join a French-Canadian club will sometimes inquire if there is an "open" English membership.

Each group has its own important events. The St Andrew's Ball for the English, the Bal des Petits Souliers for the French, and the Angels' Ball for the Jewish community are typical examples. Each has a different flavour.

"The Angels' Ball is fantastic," according to one local fashion authority. "You've never seen more opulence. And they all look exactly alike. Several years ago, when the hair was bouffant and swept to one side, the receiving line looked like a row of turn signals.

"At a Jewish event like this, the gowns are luxurious but somehow slightly vulgar. At the Bal des Petits Souliers, the gowns are not as expensive but there is much more natural elegance and greater chic. The St Andrew's Ball is the tattiest of them all. At the St George's Ball, the dresses look like left-overs from the thirties and forties. The St Patrick's Ball, of course, doesn't mean anything."

Jewish and French-Canadian women in Montreal spend lavishly on clothes. One husband who recently accompanied his wife to a large department store, not the city's most expensive, practically fainted when he came across four gowns priced at more than one thousand dollars. Imported evening gowns in the top department stores sell briskly at prices ranging from $500 to $1,500.

"In the past ten years, life in Montreal has become much more fashionable," reported a student of the city's social stratospheres.

"Now you take [a well-known hat shop] for example. I don't think she has a hat that sells for less than fifty dollars and her clientele is 99 per cent French Canadian. She sells mink hats for $250 to $300 and you see them all over the place. It's incredible."

Jewish women provide the main market for imported high fashion. French Canadians prefer to buy their dresses from Montreal couturiers who usually have studied in Paris.

"The Anglo-Saxon woman will go to a little shop that knows her," said a fashion expert. "She seems to be a little more careful, a little duller. There is less chance of her being noticed on the street.

"If Mrs [prominent Anglocrat] bought a Balenciaga at Holt's, she would have everything removed that would tend to make it stand out. A Jewish woman would add beads to it."

In their clothes sense, or lack of it, female members of the Anglostocracy reflect the mores of their tribe. In the Jewish community, money is made for display; in the French-Canadian community, for enjoyment. In the Anglostocracy, it is enough to know that it is there.

There is a story about a female member of an old and wealthy Anglocrat family who regularly took the bus home from committee meetings at the Montreal Museum of Fine Arts. During one trip she was offered a seat by a younger woman who remarked to a friend that it was "a shame that none of the men would give their seat to a charwoman who had obviously been on her feet all day."

"When one of my friends is making money, I can see it," said a Jewish businessman, "but the guy next door in Westmount dresses like a bum and drives an old Chev station wagon. You would never know that he's sitting on a pile of stock that makes me look like a piker."

It is impolite to discuss cash in the Anglostocracy. When a prominent Montreal woman died recently, leaving an estate of approximately $27 million, almost half of which went into the public domain, neither English-language newspaper in the city felt that it was worth an obituary notice.

This does not mean that money is unimportant in the Anglostocracy. The Anglocrat may drive to his office in a Volkswagen but only because he knows that other Anglocrats know that he is employing "ostentation in reverse" with dazzling effect. According to a foreigner who lived temporarily in Montreal in a position that placed him in contact with all the élite groups, money is more vital to social standing in the Anglostocracy than in French-Canadian society, which specializes to some extent in well-aged poverty. He also claimed that Anglocrats place more importance than French Canadians on a husband's profession. As long as his blood lines are good, it does not much matter what a French Canadian does; but the Anglostocracy seem to reflect some of the traditional British distaste for "trade," although some trades, such as brewing, are eminently acceptable.

In the lower income groups, French-Canadian women are reputed to exhibit the flair for colour which some authorities claim that they adopted or inherited from the Indians. There is a saying in the trade that if you have a red dress with sequins, sell it in French Canada; if you have a navy blue dress with a white collar, sell it in Ontario; if you have a grey flannel suit, sell it in Vancouver.

At the time of writing, the Parisian magazine *Elle* was said to be the fashion bible of young French-Canadian women. A small advertisement in the newspaper *Le Devoir* about the opening of an *Elle* boutique in Montreal brought about fifty girls to the shop the next morning. It was a Saturday and the shop was closed. Some of the disappointed customers made inquiries next door, where a young French-Canadian couturier was hard at work.

"All the girls looked like the editorial pages of *Elle* — a little tiny, tiny bit cheap but cute," he later told a friend.

"There is no comparable group of Anglo-Saxon girls — girls who are wild for taste like that. French-Canadian girls have a very special excitement about clothes. They can be wrong and awful but still very gay."

Social barriers between the different worlds become most apparent at the level of informal contact. It is probably true to say that a majority of English-speaking Montrealers cannot remember ever being invited to a French-Canadian home for dinner — or inviting a French Canadian to eat at their table.

A western Canadian newspaperman assigned to Montreal recalled his first innocent attempt to blend English and French at an apartment-warming party. There was an atmosphere of near-panic when representatives of both groups found themselves in a living-room too small for division into ethnic territories. The situation was complicated by a certain number of English-speaking guests who couldn't speak French and a scattering of nationalist French Canadians who refused on principle to speak English. The conversation eventually was carried on in French — an unusual occurrence in an English-French group and an interesting sign of the times. Those who could not speak French sat on the sidelines nodding and grinning as if they were at a Japanese tea party.

"Things are changing," claimed a typical Anglocrat. "Five years ago I never went inside their homes and they never came inside mine. But just the other week, I was invited to a party in a French-Canadian home where at least 25 per cent of the guests were English-speaking, including a few Jews. I must admit that it was the first time that I had seen all three groups in a private home.

"I remember my wife whispering to me, 'Good heavens, I don't know a soul here.' Finally I spotted a Jewish business friend and we made a beeline for him."

A prominent Montrealer-by-adoption said that he had as

many French as English friends. During his first few years in Montreal, he explained, he and his wife, who had lived in Paris, met no French Canadians. One day, at a resort, they complained about this lack of contact to two French-Canadian couples. The French-Canadians promised to remedy the situation, and did. A few weeks after returning to Montreal, they invited the non-Quebec couple to a large dinner party where all the guests were French Canadians. After that, all the people at the dinner party invited the couple to their homes. This obviously was a planned program of introduction to French-Canadian society. To a native Montreal Anglocrat, it must sound utterly unbelievable.

Montrealers who belong to the school of sweetness and light — a diminishing number in recent years — point to a certain number of "mixed" activities to prove that French-English-Jewish relations in Montreal are not as bad as they might seem. It is true that barriers are lowered slightly in the world of "culture," but mainly because it would be too nonsensical even in Montreal to have such things as French and English symphony orchestras. (At one time, incredible as it might sound, there were two such orchestras.)

The original group that backed the Place des Arts cultural centre contained leading members of the Jewish and French-Canadian communities and the Anglostocracy. It was a sterling example of co-operation until it made the fatal mistake of hiring a senior administrator from the United States who was bilingual in the wrong direction. He spoke Spanish. French-Canadian pickets instantly appeared outside the new concert hall. This was followed by a strike of French-Canadian entertainers. Instead of opening with the best opera festival in Canadian history, the concert hall produced a typical Quebec riot as its first attraction.

However, the fact that Samuel Bronfman, Bartlett Morgan, Louis Lapointe, and others were able to work together smoothly to build the hall is significant. There is some contact between the various worlds in Montreal at the very top level of business and in many professions. Common interests draw people together. But this contact is rarely continued when the five o'clock shadow falls over the city.

The Montreal Museum of Fine Arts is another tripartite project in the sense that members of all three groups are represented on its executive committee. As far as financial support is concerned, it is largely the child of the Anglostocracy. Most of its valuable items have come from private Anglocrat collections. Although attendance at the Museum reflects the make-up of the city's population, less than one-fifth of its four thousand members are French Canadians. French-Canadian attendance is bolstered by almost 20,000 French-Canadian school children who visit the Museum every winter under an arrangement with the Catholic School Commission. The Protestant School Commission of Greater Montreal has no similar program, being intent on providing a "practical" education for future millionaires who will be able to endow still more museums for the edification of French-Canadian children.

The Anglostocracy supports culture for the masses in a manner out of all proportion to its numerical strength in the city. It is difficult to think of large city-wide cultural institutions which are supported primarily by the French Canadians on a voluntary basis. This sort of philanthropy is an Anglo-Saxon custom. The French Canadian tends to look to government or some other official organization to do the same job. His idea of the individual citizen's rôle in a democratic society leaves relatively little room for private action and responsibility. He is inclined to let Big Brother take care of problems, regardless of whether Big Brother happens at a given moment to be wearing a French crown, a British crown, a cardinal's crimson biretta, or a politician's top hat.

The "giving" instinct of the average French Canadian has been dulled by generations of automatic contribution to the bottomless collection plate of the Roman Catholic Church.

In December, 1963, La Chambre de Commerce du District de Montréal analysed the results of the annual Prêt d'Honneur campaign sponsored by the St Jean Baptiste Society. The conclusions were published in the newsletter of the Chambre under a headline which can be translated as "We Should Blush." While 439 French-Canadian firms gave an average of $52.97 each for a total donation of $23,254, the average donation of 283 English-language firms was $118.25 for a total of $33,465.

About 99 per cent of the university students who receive loans under the Prêt d'Honneur scheme are French Canadians.

The St Jean Baptiste Parade through downtown Montreal in June, 1964, was infiltrated by a band of young separatists waving Quebec flags and torches and shouting "Québec Libre" in unison. But most of the elaborate floats in the parade, organized to honour French Canada's patron saint, were sponsored by foreign-owned or Anglocrat companies.

A great deal of philanthropic money flows from the English into the French side in Montreal. A comparative trickle moves in the opposite direction. The French Canadian always explains this by referring to an obvious fact: the amount of cash in the hands of the Anglostocracy. But there is also at least a dim recognition among the English that they owe something to the community which has enabled them to amass their wealth. Generosity and a Christian tradition of service cannot be eliminated as motives.

According to 1961-62 statistics compiled by the Canadian Welfare Council, the highest per capita contributions to united community campaigns are found among the English-speaking Protestant, English-speaking Catholic, and Jewish communities in Montreal. The Jewish contribution in Montreal of $7.50 per capita to the Jewish campaign was at the top of the Canadian list, followed by the Federation of Catholic Charities ($7.25), and Montreal's United Red Feather Services ($7.17). The per capita contribution to the Fédération des Oeuvres Canadienne-françaises in Montreal was $1.03. In Toronto the per capita contribution was $5.98 and the national average was $3.13.

Of course, these statistics have to be studied in the light of the French-Canadian contribution to religious charities.

"The English-speaking people have made a lot of mistakes but they poured a lot of money back into this city," commented an Anglocrat. "The English-speaking Montrealer is the most understanding guy in the world. He contributes more to the welfare of his community than the average citizen anywhere else in North America, in the world.

"If we weren't understanding, we wouldn't have stayed here."

Pioneer Anglocrats were usually raised in a Protestant ethic that held good works in high esteem and frowned on frivolous and expensive self-indulgence. Recalled the son of a typical specimen, "Dad's idea of living it up was to attend a Sunday School convention in Japan." Some of the city's greatest Anglocrats have been great philanthropists by any standards. In the financial year ending in the spring of 1963, McGill University's second largest single source of outside funds was the late J. W. McConnell, proprietor of the *Montreal Star*. His total donation of $1,900,000 in that year was exceeded only by Quebec government construction grants amounting to $2,500,000. The university received almost twice as much from this one individual as from the Canada Council. In recent years, wealthy members of the Jewish community have departed more and more from in-group giving to contribute generously to various projects that benefit the entire community. The Steinberg brothers, for example, have given generously to the University of Montreal where the extension department tailored a special French course for them and executives of their supermarket empire.

In art, as in clothes, the Jewish community does the handsome thing. Although Montreal still contains probably the greatest private North American collections of pre-1860 paintings outside of New York, most of them in Anglocrat homes, important art purchases now are made primarily by Jewish patrons. According to one authority, Jewish art purchases equal those made by both French-Canadian and Anglocrat patrons and "only the Jewish community does any important buying of art." He estimated that possibly two to three dozen major works of art — objects costing more than $25,000 each — arrive in Montreal every year from New York, London, and Paris and most of these are purchased by Jewish customers. He claimed that French Canadians do not easily spend more than two thousand dollars on a single work of art.

When a French Canadian does buy, almost invariably he purchases the work of a contemporary French-Canadian artist. Art supposedly knows no national boundaries, but in Quebec nationalism is a strong and insidious artistic influence. French-Canadian artists are quite popular in Toronto but the French-

Canadian public rarely returns the compliment by purchasing the work of painters in English Canada. In recent years French Canada seems to have isolated itself deliberately from the lively artistic milieu in Toronto, to its own impoverishment.

As the spirit of nationalism has grown in French Canada in the sixties, creative activity, particularly in the literary field, appears to have declined. It is almost as if the extreme concentration on nationalism had sucked up far too much intellectual and creative energy. New poets, novelists, and playwrights of exciting talent have been few and far between.

Dr Evan Turner, who returned to the United States in 1964 after five years as director of the Montreal Museum of Fine Arts, had an outsider's awareness of French-Canadian introversion and spoke about it in terms that the typical Anglocrat would consider ungentlemanly. (The First Commandment honoured by the Anglostocracy is: "Thou shalt not criticize the French Canadian — publicly.")

In a brief to the Royal Commission on Bilingualism and Biculturalism, he stated:

When the local achievement is felt to be more interesting or, even graver, more important, when standards of quality are gauged by whether one is local or foreign, then a culture is sacrificing standards and is in danger of emasculating itself.

When chauvinism is responsible, as it is repeatedly, for appraising and collecting exclusively the paintings of one's own group, whether French or English, one is certainly not gaining the full advantages of the Canadian situation. To cite a personal example, I have been told by a distinguished French-speaking artist of Montreal that, given my background, I am unable to judge and appreciate properly the achievements of French-speaking Canadian painters.

While this is certainly an extremist attitude, I have nonetheless encountered various cases when absorption in the achievement of one's group bars truly objective appreciation.

The cleavage between English and French penetrates even the intellectual élite, the one group that might be expected to rise above differences of language, religion, and social background. The University of Montreal and McGill University, on opposite sides of Mount Royal, remain separated by approximately the distance between Rome and London.

McGill University is directed by a twenty-eight-member Board of Governors. At the time of writing — changes apparently are expected in the near future — this board continues to stand as a symbol of Anglocrat exclusiveness perfected to a degree that startles even a Montrealer. Although 48 per cent of the student body at McGill University is Protestant, 24 per cent Jewish, and 15 per cent Roman Catholic, there is not a single Jew or Roman Catholic on the board. It is a hive of unadulterated WASPishness.

On the other side of Mount Royal, the rector of the University of Montreal is appointed by the Vatican. The university is controlled by a twelve-member Board of Governors, the board at the time of writing consisting of nine laymen and three Roman Catholic clergymen.

McGill students traditionally have had little contact with those at the University of Montreal and the number of separatists among the French-Canadian student body in recent years has further alienated the two groups. There is a tiny handful of professors who wander freely between the two institutions but only in the past few years have McGill and the University of Montreal discussed, in a significant way, such joint efforts as common invitations to prominent visiting professors.

"They're simply not polite at the University of Montreal," complained one member of McGill's Board of Governors.

"If we invite their students to some function here, eventually we get an acceptance couched in the usual roundabout French-Canadian terms. Then, in many instances, no one shows up."

McGill University's 1961 brief to Quebec's Royal Commission on Education contained a candid assessment of the situation:

In fact, the Western world is one, troubled but simultaneously enriched by linguistic differences. Our universities have a common heritage, to which they owe a common allegiance. One might, however, be pardoned for never suspecting this.

Between McGill and the University of Montreal there are few exchanges; their relations are literally as well as figuratively ultramontane. All of us can at once recall exceptions, but the daily rule is for us to go our separate ways. At a recent scientific congress at the University of Montreal, it was discovered that not one of the 40 McGill graduate students attending the meeting had ever previously set foot in the main buildings on Mount Royal Boulevard.

Among the many French-Canadian enclaves in Montreal which rarely feel the tread of an Anglocrat foot, City Hall is the holy of holies. Once upon a time, English-speaking politicians ran Montreal, although not as efficiently or as honestly as their present-day descendants might imagine. Writing in 1913, two years after the departure of the last English-speaking mayor, a local English-language journalist admitted that "to be quite frank, there was a long period during which the English-speaking people seemed to think that almost anybody was good enough to make an alderman."

A Royal Commission declared in 1909 that the city's administration had been "saturated with corruption" since 1892. It estimated that one-quarter of the city's revenue had been devoted to "bribes and malversations of all kinds."

Long after the last English-speaking mayor left office, the Anglostocracy continued to speak in golden tones at City Hall. Their interests were well represented by English-speaking members of council or French Canadians who had become almost members-by-adoption of the Anglostocracy. Men such as the late J. O. Asselin, Chairman of the Executive Committee during the period investigated by the famous vice probe of the 1950's, which confirmed his reputation for public service, were channels of communication between the Anglostocracy and the French Canadians who dominated civic government and the city's civil service. But this has changed under Mayor Jean Drapeau. The present government seems to manage its affairs without the guidance of a quiet English voice behind the throne.

Said an Anglocrat who had been connected with one of the many investigations into previous city governments, "I came out of the whole thing disgusted with my own people. The Anglo-Saxon community had its greatest opportunity to participate in civic government when we had 'C' category councillors. [This was a group of councillors, abolished by popular referendum in 1962, which was appointed by various organizations in the city, some of them English-speaking.]

"Our appointed representatives," he continued, "took advantage of their position to further their own community at the expense of the development of the city. And the politicians we now have at City Hall know perfectly well what went on in the old days. What sort of opinion can you expect them to have of our group? Now we can't sit down to discuss anything without them thinking: 'What are they up to?'"

Few Montrealers will dispute the fact that City Hall under the current Drapeau administration is a more antiseptic place than in the good old days of tolerated corruption.

"At that time, if you wanted something, you had to pay for it," said an Anglocrat lawyer. "You would never get an answer from City Hall. But a civil servant would show up unannounced in your office and advise you to see the agent of Mr So-and-so, the local councillor. The government did nothing, good or bad, unless it was paid to do it. We regarded it as a form of taxation."

English-speaking Montrealers usually blame the French Canadians for the old system, claiming that the English community had no choice but to conform.

"I wonder if that's really true," pondered an Anglocrat businessman with a certain experience of civic politics.

"After all, you have to ask yourself who is the biggest crook, the Anglo-Saxon millionaire who offers a bribe or the $4,000-a-year municipal clerk with ten children who accepts it?"

Members of the English-speaking community further alienated Mayor Drapeau by voting against him when he was running on his original reform platform in 1954. They appeared to be less concerned about municipal corruption than about the fact that Drapeau had been a nationalist and anti-conscription federal candidate during World War II. Only in 1962 did the English-speaking constituencies in the west end of the city give Mayor Drapeau a majority.

Six weeks before the 1960 election, Mayor Drapeau's party didn't have a single English-speaking candidate in prospect. This astounding situation might have persisted until election day had not a group of young English-speaking Montrealers, none of them particularly prominent, visited Drapeau on their own initiative to offer their support. Several were persuaded to run for office.

Montreal must be the only city in North America where the dominant economic group is practically absent from the municipal council. There was at the time of writing only one Anglo-Saxon Protestant among the forty-eight members of the council and he, a school teacher, was the result of a long and diligent search by the Drapeau party before the last election. The smaller Jewish community has four councillors. Less than one-fifth of the council is English-speaking although about one-quarter of the city's population is English-speaking. As a general rule, the turn-out of voters for municipal elections is lower in English than in French districts.

This situation is partly explained by the fact that most leading Anglocrats do business in the city of Montreal but live in such autonomous municipalities as Westmount and the Town of Mount Royal. Still, there are many prominent English-speaking Montrealers who might serve with distinction on city council were they not prevented from running for office by the prevailing Anglo-Saxon assumption that City Hall is no place for an honest man. Membership in Westmount's city council is socially acceptable but it is considered almost vulgar to be a member of the Montreal council.

English-speaking people play no important part in the civil service of either the city or the province. Referring to this situation in the Quebec civil service in a speech in August, 1964, Montreal lawyer Kenneth C. Mackay said that "it springs not from a lack of interest in the civil service on the part of English-speaking people but from a closed-door policy — involuntary, possibly, but none the less real — which has been more and more evident for some years." One example of this, he said, was the disappearance of a tradition which had reserved certain judicial appointments for English-speaking Quebeckers.

The English-speaking community's aloofness from civic politics can only make it more difficult for the two main groups in the city to work together. Already there has been one important illustration of this. In 1964 the Drapeau-Saulnier administration was making every effort to promote its policy of a single civic administration for the Island of Montreal to replace the present patchwork of independent municipalities. Some of the strongest objections to this policy were coming from municipalities dominated by English-speaking people and the "racial" implications were beginning to fascinate citizens more than the legitimate arguments on each side. There were no influential English-speaking voices in the City of Montreal to oppose or support the policy and to remove the impression that it was an attempt by "French" Montreal to grab Westmount and other wealthy English-speaking municipalities.

The Anglostocracy's refusal to serve at City Hall as spokesmen for a minority group, and its inability to purchase influence there as it once did, means that the destiny of the city for the first time is being shaped by French-Canadian politicians aware primarily of the interests of their own group.

4

❧

Business and Biculturalism

In any society a business aristocracy tries to perpetuate itself
against the exterior threat of new young blood bubbling with
ambition, and the inner threat of old tired blood diluted by
double martinis. This effort is most apparent when the new
blood springs from a different stock, as it does in Quebec.

Some indication of the French-Canadian's position in the
business aristocracy in Quebec can be gained from Professor
John Porter's research on economic élites in Canada. Unfortunately for this author, Professor Porter's comprehensive work
on the subject was in the process of publication when this
book was being written. However, he published a preliminary
report on his work in 1957 in the *Canadian Journal of Economics and Political Science*.

Professor Porter, who is on the faculty at Carleton University in Ottawa, selected as his élite in 1957 a group of 907
Canadian resident directors of 170 dominant corporations.
These 907 men shared 1,304 of the 1,613 directorships in the
dominant corporations, 119 of the 203 directorships in the
nine chartered banks of the day, and 78 of the 134 directorships in the 10 largest Canadian life insurance companies. To
this group he added seventy-eight directors of the chartered
banks who did not hold directorships in the dominant corporations. He was successful in collecting data on 760 of this group
of 985 titans.

Professor Porter discovered that only 6.7 per cent of this
élite could be classified as French Canadian, although French
Canadians form roughly one-third of the national population.

Of the French-Canadian élite, one-third were lawyers and fourteen others "have important political affiliations."

Only 10 per cent of the élite was Roman Catholic, although Roman Catholics form more than 40 per cent of the Canadian population.

"As far as ethnic background is concerned," Professor Porter concluded, "it is clear that preference is given to English-speaking persons of British origin in recruitment to the economic élite."

This preference is quite natural in the sense that members of any group normally tend to assist one another, particularly if they are members of the same family group. This is, if anything, more prevalent in French Canada than in English Canada, the difference being that in English Canada there has been more to assist with.

Of the 611 members of the élite who were born in Canada, 22 per cent inherited their positions directly from near kin. More than one-third of the élite came from families already well-established in the upper classes. Professor Porter gave a maximum estimate of 18 per cent for the proportion who had worked their way up from the bottom of the social ladder. He refined his élite into a super-élite of one hundred "most powerful" men. Of the eighty-eight who were Canadian-born, 30 per cent had kinfolk, usually fathers, in the economic élite. Only 15 per cent had climbed from lower social levels up to the super-élite.

The Porter portrait is highly discouraging to an ambitious French Canadian. He belongs to a group which occupies only 6.7 per cent of the élite positions in the country — the figure might be slightly higher today than in 1957 — and is faced with the undeniable fact that the élite tends to be a self-perpetuating group.

It is currently being drummed into French Canadians that all they require to get ahead in business is better education. But of the executives in financial institutions studied by Professor Porter, less than half had university training. The élite included twenty-three executives of chartered banks and only one of these men was university-trained. If it is primarily his lack of education which makes a French Canadian unfit for

the business world, then Canadian banks, with highly uned-
ucated men in their top positions, must be in a parlous state.

Education is not some sort of magic pill which, when di-
gested by French Canadians, will turn them into super-élite-
men overnight. Creating "Francocrats" is not that easy. It is
a process affected by social attitudes and emotional prejudices.

The average Anglocrat shies away from the word "emotion"
as if it were spelled with four letters. When he talks about
emotional French Canadians, he does it with a touch of superiority. He would be astounded to discover that many French
Canadians today regard *him* as a highly emotional creature.

"If only the English-speaking businessmen would try to look
at what we're doing in practical terms," complained a civil
servant in René Lévesque's Department of Natural Resources
in Quebec City. "Every time we make a move, they get all
excited. They see everything as some sort of horrible plot
against them."

In a northern Quebec mining community, the small English-
speaking element employed by a national corporation set up
a fearful racket when the company decided to fly a Quebec
provincial flag beside the Red Ensign in front of the plant.

"Don't talk to me about the unemotional English after that
business," said a French-Canadian executive who had been
involved in the controversy.

Another French-Canadian executive in a large national company with headquarters in Montreal remarked, "When the
English-speaking percentage of management drops from 93 to
92 per cent, all the English executives look worried and start
to talk about leaving. It's a scream."

"I've given a lot of thought to this," said a member of a
bluer-than-blue Montreal Anglocrat family. And he had, as it
became evident during a three-hour interview in the board-
room of one of his family's many enterprises.

"You can divide both the French and English camps into
three groups," he said.

"In the French-Canadian camp the first group is what you
might call the élite — the curés, the old-line politicians, judges,
and so forth. They think that the English are okay. They've
worked well with them. The second French group is the busi-

ness or industrial group, men from thirty to fifty years of age. They're the ones who are seriously concerned with what's happening. Then there's the third group, the young French Canadians. They're afire today and there's someone fanning their tails all the time to keep that fire going.

"In the English camp, the first group is made up of those who are totally against the French Canadian. Anything a French Canadian says or does is wrong. There is a second group whose members feel that the French Canadian has been reasonably well treated but, for a variety of reasons, all his own fault, has failed to perform.

"These two groups form the majority in the English camp. But there is another, smaller group — those who feel that the French Canadian has been shabbily treated.

"As far as I'm concerned, members of this third group are the only ones who are attempting to make important changes. The others are going in for such insane operations as trying to make men of fifty learn French and running around trying to find French Canadians for their boards. That's not what the French Canadians want.

"What the French Canadian wants is an equal chance to get ahead. This is what he hasn't had. The English-speaking Quebecker who doesn't admit any fault on the English side, who doesn't admit that there's been discrimination in business against the French Canadian, isn't going to change.

"The number two group, the industrial or commercial group, is the most important on the French side. They have the knowledge and ability and the willingness to work and they are unhappy to see on the English side a failure to understand the problem. They know that the French Canadian wants only the same chance as his English counterpart.

"If there had only been more opportunity for these men in the past to hold senior positions, we wouldn't be having all this trouble today. Of course now there's a mad scramble to get these fellows and they're not easy to find. So you get outfits like —— appointing men like —— as vice-presidents. That's not impressing anyone. They shouldn't have brought him in from outside but should have found a French Canadian who had worked his way up inside the company."

This particular Anglocrat claimed that he had started to groom French Canadians for senior positions within one of his own enterprises in the mid-1940's.

"There was no apparent change in the company up to 1954," he recalled. "We had, as always, an English-speaking top man, three English-speaking senior men, and a totally French-Canadian staff of salesmen. I realized that it was wrong. All we were doing was using the French Canadians to bring business to us.

"I remember our old vice-president and general manager saying to me one day, 'Never hire a French Canadian as an office boy because an office boy can become president. Only hire them as salesmen.' It was the same everywhere. In the banks, the railways, most of the large corporations. They were all English at the top.

"It wasn't hard to see that the French Canadians were getting fed up. Their system of education was always thrown up at them, but the argument about education doesn't stand up when you look at the way French Canadians have operated their own businesses and particularly at the way they have moved ahead in the professions.

"Then there was the Catholic religion. I've known English-speaking Quebeckers who claimed that confession encouraged French Canadians to steal because, if they stole, they just had to go to confession and everything was all right.

"English-speaking Quebeckers maintained as a rule that French Canadians couldn't be incorporated into a business or given senior rank. Well, I thought otherwise. Today this company of mine that I mentioned has no English-speaking people at all in its top ranks. And since we started to make the change-over in 1954, our profits have doubled.

"Of course I did a lot of work with these men, helping them to get to know the tradition and policy of the company. But now they've taken charge. The other day, they bought an independent company for us practically on their own hook. They worked out the whole deal and all I had to do was give the final okay. They came up with a more astute analysis of the local situation than any English-speaking person could have produced.

"Now you take another one of our companies. The men in charge there still belong to the 'there'll-always-be-a-Westmount' school. And today they're being licked left and right by the French-Canadian competition.

"I've been severely criticized for doing what I've done, even by members of my own family. I was at a party recently and the president of a large outfit here came up to me and said, 'So you're the one that likes the French-speaking people, eh?' And then he started to say, 'Look, I know the French Canadians, I was born and brought up with them. . . .'

"Then I got mad. I said to him, 'You're lying. And people like you are the cause of all the trouble. Just because you were born in ———, Quebec, and your mother parked your pram next to a French-Canadian baby in the park, or you had a French-Canadian maid, you think you understand the French Canadians. Why, you've never really seen a French Canadian since the day you were born.

"'In other parts of Canada you go around telling people that you know the French Canadians when you don't know them at all. But these people don't know that. They accept you as some sort of authority.'"

Said another Anglocrat in Montreal: "I think that we could have done a lot more to bring them along with us economically, without affecting our profits. All the huge head offices in Montreal could have had at least six French Canadians on their boards without any detrimental effect on their operations.

"In a few generations they would have learned a lot from us. Around the table — that's where the money's made. We could have found them if we had looked. It doesn't take any brains to be a director of a company.

"Some of the English still don't catch on. They're all trying to put the same Joe on their boards. And of course it's the fault of the French Canadians too. Maybe the few who were accepted were happy to keep it that way. Maybe they didn't push hard to get more French Canadians into the group."

Like most convenient labels, "Anglostocracy" is far too sweeping a term. In business, the Anglostocracy breaks down into two distinct groups. The first contains what one Montreal businessman called "the fur traders." They are the descendants of the original breed of capitalists. Behind them, in some cases, lie generations of wealth, business influence, and social prestige. The second group is the new generation of managers who run banks, railways, airlines, and many of the largest corporations. In this group power and wealth rarely go back a generation. The hand at the helm today was only yesterday wielding a spanner or pushing a teller's pen.

In the past twenty-five years or so, the first group, with some exceptions, has been diminishing and the second group expanding as an important force in the Quebec economy. This has had results both good and bad because it is in the first group that one encounters both the best understanding and the most complete ignorance of the French-Canadian situation.

An intelligent Old Montreal Anglocrat has a far keener appreciation of French-Canadian problems than any non-Quebecker. A stupid one is a frightening mixture of inherited prejudice. In the past few years, it was a general rule that the more recently an English-speaking executive had arrived in Montreal from points outside Quebec, the more terrified he was by all the noise generated by the separatists. One can accuse the native Anglocrats of being smug but there was a certain stability in their approach which sometimes led to a calmer and more accurate appraisal of the long-range situation. It was quite common in the early 1960's to hear imported Anglocrats saying, "*If* Quebec separates. . . ." This "if" never passed the lips of most old-family Anglocrats.

As one of them remarked, "Just because you get some character in long hair with a year or two in Paris and an article published in *Parti Pris* [a small separatist magazine] . . . *that* doesn't touch the soul of the people here.

"You always have the fringy type," he snorted, "but I don't think that their masquerade can have a deep-seated effect. It's as if the English-speaking people here suddenly started to organize fox-hunts and cricket matches. Only the faddists go in for that sort of thing."

New Anglocrats imported from other provinces or the United States can regard the prospect of being booted out of

Quebec with a certain sang-froid. After all, they can always go home. But for the native Anglocrat and his lesser English-speaking brethren, home is Quebec. Be it ever so troubled, there's no other place.

"You can't simply say, 'Out!' to one million people," is a typical comment.

New Anglocrats almost invariably are "progressive" in their approach to French Canadians. But the goodwill is worth very little if it is based, as it often is, on ignorance.

A typical example was the president of a large national corporation, one of the biggest in Canada, who would be shocked to hear himself described as anti-French Canadian. Yet his interpretation of history in Quebec is so totally different from the prevailing French-Canadian view that he cannot possibly understand the basic reasons behind the unrest in Quebec.

"The reasons," he said, "are education, religion, and inherited characteristics. The French Canadians have had equal opportunities. But they weren't interested in business.

"For two hundred years, the Anglo-Saxon has tried to give Quebec what it wanted. There was no oppression after the Conquest. Have you ever thought about what would have happened if Germans or Japanese had triumphed on the Plains of Abraham? They would have liquidated the French Canadians.

"Now, all of a sudden, the French Canadians expect someone to hand them everything on a platter. They claim that they have been depressed and held down. I would like to know — by whom? They've had every democratic right that every Canadian had."

This man, in charge of a company that is a major employer in Canada, had spent his entire working life with this opinion fixed solidly in his mind — an opinion at variance with the views of practically every French Canadian in the country. The tragedy of the separation between English and French in Quebec was illustrated by the fact that never in his life, according to his own recollection, had he discussed this interpretation of history with a French Canadian in a personal and informal way. He had no personal French-Canadian friends — in fact, according to him, few friends at all.

"That's a hobby that some people enjoy," he said. "I'm not much on the social side of life."

At the end of the interview he was asked if, in his opinion, English-speaking Canadians were to blame at all for the discontent in Quebec.

"That's a difficult question," he said. "I think that there has been narrow-minded prejudice on our part. It certainly hasn't helped the situation."

On the spur of the moment, however, he was unable to think of any concrete examples of this prejudice.

Despite all their goodwill, most of Quebec's new Anglocrats simply do not understand the situation. Most of them are unable to read French-language newspapers. Few have personal friends on the French-Canadian side. They do not get accurate reflections of French-Canadian opinion from the young French-Canadian assistants that many have hired. The French Canadians that they meet in the course of business are of their own age and income group and usually not representative of their people.

"It's hard to tell what you mean by French-Canadian friends," said one of the most important men in Canadian banking. "The people that I see are pretty Anglicized. Take Senator ———, for example. I don't even think of him as being French Canadian.

"Most of my French-Canadian friends seem to be as appalled as I am at the crazy events. But they don't speak out when they're with other French Canadians."

Whatever their shortcomings, the new Anglocrats are the most influential element of Quebec's business aristocracy. Said the same banker, "The 'fur traders' are of diminishing importance. If you surveyed the directors of businesses in Montreal, you might get 15 per cent who were born here. The rest of us are here only because we happen to work for companies whose head offices happen to be in Montreal."

"Many of the old families have practically disappeared as far as real money is concerned," admitted a native Anglocrat.

"We haven't done what we could have done in the past twenty-five years. You should go to Toronto and see what they're doing, or to Calgary or Vancouver. It makes us look pretty decadent. Sometimes I think that it's a good thing that the French Canadians are trying to replace us. At least they're hungry."

"The pattern has been for wealth to die out in a few generations," said another. "Too much drinking.

"If you traced the descendants of the financial powers of the 1890's, you wouldn't find many today in positions of authority although some might still have a considerable amount of money.

"There is a certain lassitude at the moment among the Anglo-Saxon group. It is sensitive to its loss of political power."

"The Anglo-Saxon group is twice-castrated," said an authority on the city's financial world.

"First, they let the Americans get ahead of them. Then they let Toronto forge ahead. Some Montreal people are trying to adapt, but the rest are doing exactly what Duplessis did — going into a tent and hiding. If they discriminate today, it's because they're basically insecure. They're trying to hang onto a dwindling situation. They're afraid of competition because most of them have never done anything creative. Even when a member of their own group tries to do something, they want to cut his throat.

"I remember when young ——— broke away from the firm of ——— and ——— and tried to get a seat for himself on the Exchange. The old firm set out to kill him, and he barely made it."

A young executive on St James Street said, "Before 1935, the Montreal Exchange was the most important in the country. But it was dominated by an older group. The people in the Toronto Exchange were younger and more aggressive. When outside capital was looking for speculative investment in Canada, the Montreal people weren't interested in taking risks or breaking new ground. They were selling a few established stocks. They failed to realize what outside investors were after. And the blood was dripping right out of the market here. The turning-point came about 1947 and by 1959 Montreal had something like one-quarter of the national market.

"The old families never acquired a competitive instinct.

They never built for the sake of building. Now they're on the defensive. They're a drag on the whole community."

The English-French division in the business community is reflected formally in the existence of two parallel businessmen's organizations, the Montreal Board of Trade and La Chambre de Commerce du District de Montréal. The Board of Trade traces its origin to a Committee of Trade founded in 1822. Although the Board was set up "to watch over the general interests of the trade and the country, and to advance and render prosperous the lawful trade and commerce of this province and of the city of Montreal more especially," without reference to whether merchants were situated east or west of St Lawrence Boulevard, the organization inevitably was controlled by the dominant English-speaking business group.

In 1866, a group of French-speaking businessmen organized a schism which produced La Chambre.

Comparing current memberships in the two groups is difficult because each has a different system. The Board accepts only companies as members. It had 2,809 members in 1964. La Chambre has individual members — 3,500 in 1964, according to its own estimate — and more than 400 corporation members. In 1963-64, the Board received $160,771 in membership fees compared with $147,907 in membership fees paid to La Chambre. But investment income and revenue from its downtown building — La Chambre has no building of its own — gave the Board more than twice La Chambre's annual revenue in 1963-64.

The 1963-64 annual report of the Board of Trade contains one of those platitudinous paragraphs which always warm the hearts of English-speaking Canadians: "Here in Quebec, the English-speaking community perhaps has the prime responsibility and obligation to act as a medium through which the two cultures which founded Canada can resolve their misunderstandings and differences in a manner which will confirm the union so vital to the continuing growth and prosperity of the country as a whole."

Sheer poetry. But it does not camouflage the fact that there is precious little co-operation between the two organizations except in such matters as joint approaches to government. Significantly, the only specific attempt during the year to translate the reverberating paragraph into action was made by the Montreal Junior Board of Trade in co-operation with La Chambre de Commerce des Jeunes du District de Montréal. The two junior-executive groups sponsored "Operation-Rapprochement" in the spring of 1964, a one-day seminar on French-English relations in the business world.

At the time of writing, both organizations are going through a typical song-and-dance about the possibility of moving together into a new building in downtown Montreal.

"Some of our members are afraid that if we go together into the same building, it will be a step toward fusion," said an official of La Chambre.

"You might say that our members are in favour of the move intellectually but there is a strong emotional reluctance."

Would both groups benefit from the use of common dining, lounge, and office facilities?

"Not at all," said the horrified official. "Everything would be separate. Wine in one dining-room, whisky in the other. Different decor. Maybe different uniforms on the waiters."

With all its faults, and despite itself, the native Anglostocracy in Montreal has accomplished something positive. It has almost committed suicide. Or, to be more accurate, it has created the very conditions which now threaten its existence.

The industries founded by Anglocrat money and ambition, the municipal services initiated for the most part by Anglocrats, the emergence of Montreal as a financial and manufacturing colossus in a relatively underdeveloped province — all these have required thousands of labourers, tradesmen, technicians, white-collar workers, clerks, and other members of an urban proletariat. In other Canadian cities, overseas immigration provided many of these workers. In Montreal, because industrial activity boomed during both world wars, because the province received few immigrants in relation to Ontario, and because there were few rival centres of industrial activity in the province to attract surplus population from poor areas, the new proletariat was drawn to a great extent from rural Quebec.

There emerged a new urban élite which scarcely resembled the old clerical-legal-political élite which had dominated village society in French Canada and which had learned to live harmoniously and securely with the Anglocrats. The new élite included university professors, newspaper and magazine writers and editors, television and radio producers, historians, economists, and sociologists, and a new generation of French-Canadian capitalists just beginning to push against the restraints imposed by the Anglocrats. It is this group, created by the Anglocrats, which threatens the existence of the Anglostocracy, not to mention Confederation.

Sociologists can fill volumes analysing this movement and its effects, but this is the way an Anglocrat lawyer summed it up over a drink in one of his clubs:

"At one time the French Canadians were mainly down on the farm and we simply didn't meet them. But during the two wars the federal government directed them off the land and into the cities, and that's why I think we're in for a lot of violence.

"What is reasonable, bucolic horseplay in a rural area becomes something quite different when you get two or three thousand people demonstrating in a city."

A fact seldom appreciated by English-speaking Canadians is that their group in Quebec has been losing ground for almost a hundred years.

The shift from English to French majorities in the Eastern Townships, which has already been mentioned, started about 1861. There, according to a study published in 1954 by McGill University sociologist Aileen D. Ross, "English Canadians have become increasingly hostile to, and afraid of the French, for they feel that the movement of the French Canadians into the Townships is a well-organized scheme to push them out completely."

"In fact," Dr Ross stated, "neither the French nor the English understand the underlying processes which have caused their changed positions. Nor do they understand that group hostility tends to strengthen with increased competition, particularly when two groups differ so markedly from each other that the one can be clearly identified by the other.

"Language, religion, outlook and mode of life keep the French and English in the Townships so far apart that each group feels its own identity strongly, and there are few signs of assimilation. In fact, the English seldom identify themselves with the French even when there are too few of them left in a community to make a satisfactory life of their own."

The same thing has happened in Quebec City. In 1851, the British-origin group formed about one-third of the Quebec City population. According to the 1961 census, there are today only 14,000 Quebec City residents who give English as their mother tongue, out of a total population of 331,000. There are but 5,600 people in Quebec City who speak English only, compared with 243,000 who speak only French. Between 1941 and 1961 the English mother-tongue group in Quebec City grew by only 5,000 people while the French mother-tongue element acquired an additional 174,000 "souls" — to use a rather nice French term.

"The battle is over in Quebec City," said a Montreal Anglocrat with business connections in both cities.

"The French Canadians either own or run all the businesses there except for the paper companies.

"The English-speaking Quebecker, when the battle was being lost, didn't make an effort to keep his position. That is why there are few signs of unrest in Quebec City today. The French Canadians have taken it back.

"Except for a few isolated towns where everything centres about a single industry owned by English-speaking people, the only place in Quebec where the English-speaking Canadian is still powerful is Montreal. And the English here are unaware of the forces that are gathering against them."

Up against the same sort of discrimination in business that irks French Canadians in Montreal, some members of the English-speaking community in Quebec City are extremely bitter today, not only against French Canadians but against English-speaking Montrealers who have remained totally uninterested in the fate of their brethren in other parts of the province.

The Bank of Montreal provides a good illustration of the change-over in Quebec City. About twenty-five years ago, in its main Quebec City office, the manager, his two assistants, and the chief accountant were all English-speaking. Four of the bank's seven branch managers were English. Today the bank's top man in Quebec City is a French Canadian, an assistant general manager. The manager of the local main office is French Canadian, his chief accountant is French Canadian, as is one of his two assistants Only one of the bank's twelve branch managers in Quebec City is English-speaking by origin, and he is stationed at the Château Frontenac where most of the customers are English-speaking tourists.

Of course, Montreal is a "last stand" of no mean dimensions for the Custers of the Anglostocracy. In Quebec City the French Canadians were attacking a local English-speaking settlement cut off from outside reinforcements, a curious reversal in commercial life of the military situation of the French in Quebec City in 1759. While most of the English-speaking "troops" have surrendered, the fortress is still owned to a significant extent by English-speaking interests.

In Montreal, the French Canadian faces a totally different situation. Because the city contains the head offices of many national corporations, and the Canadian head offices of many foreign-owned companies operating in Canada, English-speaking business ranks are reinforced continually by executive imports from other parts of Canada, the United States, and other countries. The new arrivals from Canada and the United States are, almost to a man, unilingual, and this situation will remain unchanged until the distant time when schools in other provinces are producing bilingual graduates.

Three or four years ago, there was a sudden hope in Montreal that improved "crash courses" in French could produce bilingualism in middle-aged executives. This hope has died slowly but surely. By the summer of 1964 there were signs that the learn-French fad was disappearing rapidly.

One national corporation, more cautious than some, enrolled a selected group of fifteen executives in a twelve-week, three-hours-a-day, intensive French course in the winter of 1963-64. One month after completing the course, all fifteen said that they were disappointed by the results. They had been led to believe that the course would give them what is euphemistically described as a "working knowledge" of French. But they discovered, of course, that twelve weeks of hard work only gave them a crude foundation of vocabulary and grammar. Attempts to converse in French remained slow, laborious, and embarrassing. None of them was using French in his office and all were quickly losing what little they had learned during the course.

Chuckled a fairly bilingual Anglocrat in another company, "I have to laugh at friends of mine, coming down in the elevators at seven o'clock in the evening because they've stayed behind to take their French lessons. They always look very sheepish about it.

"They haven't got a hope of learning French at their age. I hope that the fad does decline. It isn't good for their companies to have them wasting all that time, although I suppose it's good for their own souls."

Said the president of a national corporation, "I tried twice to learn French. I was in Quebec a great deal before being posted here permanently in 194—. I saw a lot of French Canadians and I liked them. I asked myself: Why the hell shouldn't I learn French? I hired the best teachers in the country.

"But," he pounded his desk with his fist, "the demands of my job came first. In the past twenty years, it has been much more important to me that I ran a good company that could pay high wages and employ a good many people. It seemed to me that this was more important than that I should deduct time from my duties to learn French."

"Why should I spend long hours learning French when I have no opportunity to use it?" asked a bank president who confessed that French speeches on public occasions pass over him "like some sort of dream that I don't understand."

"If I had spent all my time learning French," he continued, "I wouldn't have been as good a banker and I prefer to be the best banker that I can be.

"It's true that many of our executives are learning French today. When I try to contact them on the phone, they always seem to be taking their French lessons. I can't help wondering if a customer is also trying to get them. Maybe we're losing business. And anyway, where are they going to use all this French? Not around here."

The fad for French impressed English-speaking Canadians much more than French Canadians. The French knew from personal experience the long, tough road to bilingualism. They also knew, at least the more sensible ones did, that executive-level business in most large companies based in Montreal would always be carried on in English. Most French Canadians do not resent having to be bilingual to operate at these levels. They do resent what they feel is an assumption by English-speaking executives that a thousand-word French vocabulary somehow gives them more moral right to occupy their positions. For the young French Canadian the issue is more opportunity, not more bilingual Anglo-Saxon executives.

English-speaking Canadians, even in Quebec, are confused about the whole question of bilingualism. Certainly the French Canadian wants to deal with the federal civil service in his own language; wants radio, television, and education in his own language, inside and outside Quebec; wants more opportunity to work in French at the local levels of industry and business where there is no particular reason why a French-Canadian machine operator, for instance, should have to communicate with his foreman in English; but he does not imagine that the head office of the Bank of Montreal is suddenly going to start operating bilingually at all levels. Even the separatists are quite practical about this. At the annual convention of the Rassemblement pour l'Indépendance Nationale in the spring of 1964, a resolution that would have required all industries in Quebec to have at least 60 per cent of their personnel French-speaking was rejected as "simply unrealistic because some industries may be in a position to hire 90 per cent French personnel while others may not be able to hire 25 per cent because of the lack of training of our people in some fields."

The learn-French fad is significant only because it denotes a change in the attitudes of English-speaking businessmen which should produce, in time, improvements in teaching French in elementary and secondary schools. A businessman who spends three hours a day trying to learn French is not going to object if his local school board decides to spend more money on French instruction, or if, at some time in the future, it wants to abandon the idiotic custom in Quebec which prevents English Protestant schools from hiring French-speaking Catholic teachers and vice versa.

For years to come, the French Canadian in Montreal will have to live with a business Anglostocracy recruited to a great extent outside Quebec, an Anglostocracy that still has a potent effect on the future of the French-Canadian group.

"There are four or five people who have held this province together," claimed an Anglocrat financier.

"When the last big provincial bond issue was being marketed in the United States, I received a call from a few friends in New York. The calls were very informal. The people in New York had been reading a lot of alarming things about Quebec in the newspapers. They just wanted to know how I felt about the situation.

"If I had given them a bad picture — it wouldn't have been truthful to do so, of course — but if I had given them a bad picture, they would have told their friends, and in a few days the most important people in the United States financial world would have known about it. And there would have been no money for Quebec, or only some very expensive money.

"I learned later that three or four of my friends here received the same call. A few wrong words from us and the Lesage government would have had real problems."

The Anglocrat today, in most cases, is consciously attempting to make more room for French Canadians in the business world, partly because it is good "public relations" and partly because there are more ambitious and qualified young French Canadians pounding on his door. In many large companies in Quebec at the moment, there is in fact discrimination in favour of French Canadians. There have even been cases where bilingual French Canadians have failed to get good jobs because their names were English, inherited in all likelihood from long-forgotten British soldiers. After years of discrimination against French Canadians, the pendulum has swung almost too far in the other direction.

This raises, incidentally, an interesting speculation. If young

English-speaking Montrealers decide that their language and racial background are handicaps in Quebec, will they decide to move elsewhere to find competition on equal terms? And will this mean that the "French-Canadianizing" of business in Montreal will start to snowball, as it did in Quebec City in the past twenty-five years? Will the Anglostocracy end up some day in a strong ownership position but holding relatively few of the executive jobs?

These are not questions which can be answered now. The only aspect of the situation that is certain is that more French Canadians are moving into better business positions in Montreal and that this is producing not only a shift of power toward the French-Canadian group but a radically new kind of French Canadian.

5

❧

The World Between

Unlike their Anglo-Saxon neighbours, Jews in Montreal instinctively knew what to make of separatism — a joke.

There are two kinds of Jews in Quebec, they said — the op-
timists, who are teaching their children French, and the pes-
simists, who are teaching them Hebrew. But they laughed
quietly, among themselves, and only because the Jewish sense
of humour is irrepressible. In fact, they regard separatism as
no joke. Refugees or descendants of refugees from oppression
in Europe, victims of nationalist fervour in the old countries,
they are highly allergic to the growing spirit of nationalism
evident in the quiet revolution. In their minds, political slogans of the "Maître Chez Nous" type veer dangerously close
to a philosophy which would tolerate discrimination against
non-French-Canadian groups in Quebec.

Those who have lived in Canada for some time recall the vir-
ulent anti-semitism of fascist-nationalist movements in French
Canada before World War II. At that time, scurrilous French-
language newspapers viciously attacked prominent Jewish citizens, echoing the slanders that were appearing in the Nazi
press in Europe. Two Jewish members of the Legislative Assembly were followed through the streets of Quebec City by
hooligans shouting, "A bas les Juifs." Until the post office put
a stop to it, some French Canadians were stamping slogans
on envelopes urging a boycott of Jewish merchants.

There have been no comparable outbreaks of anti-semitism
in the "new Quebec." But the trend of events during the quiet
revolution once again has impressed on Jewish Quebeckers

the fact that they belong to neither the English nor the French group in the province. They are trapped in a middle position which is familiar but none the more comfortable for that.

A tremor of apprehension ran through the Jewish community in the spring of 1964 when Natural Resources Minister René Lévesque, in his usual blunt fashion, accused the Jewish group in Quebec of gravitating "to where the strength lay, and that was to the English." In the same speech to a Jewish audience in Montreal, he urged Jewish Quebeckers to become "as close to the French Canadians as you are to English Canadians so you won't be caught in the middle, as you have been in your past history."

This was a dangerous over-simplification. The history of the province indicates that the Jews in fact have been far more successful than Anglo-Saxons in co-existing with the French Canadians. In the field of retail business they have shown little of the Anglostocracy's hesitancy to invade areas that are strictly French-speaking. Many of them speak French, despite the fact that it is for them a third or even a fourth language.

More than 35 per cent of the Jewish community in Montreal speaks both English and French, according to statistics published in 1964 in the French-language Jesuit magazine *Rélations*. This is almost equal to the 40 per cent rate of bilingualism among the city's French Canadians. About 34 per cent of the citizens of Italian origin speak both French and English and bilingualism is found among about one-third of Ukrainians, Poles, and people of Asiatic origin in Montreal. Only 27 per cent of Montrealers of British origin are bilingual and the ratio is even lower for citizens of German and Dutch origin.

It is partly by historical accident that the Jews adhere primarily to the English-speaking group in Quebec. Under the French régime, Jewish immigration to the New World was specifically forbidden, although the French colony here depended largely on merchandise and ships supplied by Abraham Gradis, a Jewish merchant of Bordeaux. One of the few Jews to set foot in the colony was a twenty-year-old girl, Esther Brandeau, who boarded a Quebec-bound ship in France in 1738 disguised as a young Christian gentleman. When her true identity was discovered the good nuns in Quebec desperately tried to convert her to Catholicism, but they had even less success with Esther than with the Indians. However there is some doubt as to whether her steadfastness was due to religious conviction alone. Because she remained Jewish and therefore ineligible to stay in Quebec, King Louis XV of France was forced to supply the money for her passage back to France.

Esther Brandeau was not only the first official Jewish immigrant to Canada but also one of the most interesting. It shows great lack of imagination on Quebec's part that her year-long residence in New France has been allowed to vanish almost completely from memory. She was quite a *cause célèbre* during her lifetime.

"Her conduct has not been wholly bad," admitted the intendant of the day in Quebec in a letter to his minister in France, "but she is so frivolous that at different times she has been both obedient and obstinate with regard to the instruction the priests desired to give her."

After the Conquest, Jews began to arrive in Quebec from England and the British colonies along the Atlantic coast. Today the Jewish community in the province, numbering almost 105,000 people according to the "religious denomination" section of the 1961 census, is somewhat smaller than Ontario's but far more important historically and in terms of relative numbers in Quebec. In the first volume of his detailed *History of the Jews in Canada* — a mine of information that I am helping myself to liberally — Benjamin G. Sack states that the first synagogue in Canada was founded in Montreal in 1768, only eight years after the Conquest. By 1851, more than 60 per cent of the Jews in Upper and Lower Canada lived in Montreal and Quebec City.

Mr Sack's history gives an indication of the active part played by Jews in the financial and public life of the province after the Conquest. In some fields, particularly in finance, their rôle seems to have been less restricted in the nineteenth century than in the twentieth.

Jacob Henry Joseph (1814-1907), a Jewish Montrealer, was director of a number of banks, president of the Montreal Gas

Company, a founder of the People's Telegraph Company, one of the first directors of the Great North West Telegraph Company, and connected with one of the first railways to be built in Canada, the Champlain-St Lawrence line which went into service in 1836. His brother, Abraham Joseph of Quebec City (1815-1886), was president of the Quebec Board of Trade, president of the Stadacona Bank, and director of La Banque Nationale. Moses Hart founded his own bank in Montreal which issued its own currency from 1835 to 1847.

David David (1764-1824) was one of the founders of the Bank of Montreal and a charter member of the Montreal Board of Trade. In the 1860's, Henry Judah was president of the Montreal City and District Savings Bank. Toward the end of the last century, Jules Helbronner, an Alsatian Jew, was editor of the city's leading French-language newspaper, *La Presse*.

Moses Judah Hays was named chief of police in Montreal in 1845 and held the post for sixteen years until his death in 1861. The first Jewish mayor in Canada was William Hyman, elected in 1851 in the tiny Gaspé village of Cap des Rosiers.

There have been few parallels in this century to the Jewish bankers and utility promoters who flourished in Montreal in the last century. It is only since the end of World War II that both the Bank of Montreal and the Royal Bank of Canada have invited Jews to membership on their boards of directors. Jews are notably absent from membership in the Montreal Stock Exchange to this day.

"The absence of Jews from banking and finance is due partly to discrimination," admitted one bank president, "but also due to the fact that a Jew does not like to do business with a Jewish bank manager. He prefers a gentile."

During the past fifty-odd years, Jewish businessmen in the province concentrated on retail business, light manufacturing, the clothing trade and, more recently and spectacularly, real-estate development. In this last field, Jews who had capital and a shrewd gambling instinct were able to operate without restriction. Some impressive Jewish fortunes were made in Montreal during the real-estate boom of the fifties and it is probably true that a majority of the huge downtown apartment blocks that have been built in the sixties are owned by Jews, although much of the capital has been provided by gentile trust companies.

The Jewish community attracts attention in Quebec because, like the English and French worlds, it is physically isolated.

There are about twenty-six Jewish communities in Ontario but only three in Quebec — in Montreal, Quebec City, and Sherbrooke — Montreal's being by far the largest. While posh residential districts are no longer out of bounds for Jews in Montreal, and almost one out of every ten Westmounters is now Jewish, they tend to live in specific areas. There is still a fairly sizable Jewish settlement in the vicinity of the old "ghetto" in the Park Avenue district, just below the northeast shoulder of Mount Royal. In the first half of this century large numbers of Jews moved into the middle-class Snowdon area of the City of Montreal. They continued to move west in the fifties and sixties into what had been, before World War II, a semi-rural French-Canadian parish. Côte St Luc, where a synagogue was the first religious building to be erected in the postwar period, has since been nicknamed the "Golden Ghetto" by its more flippant inhabitants. Even within districts such as Côte St Luc, school surveys show that certain streets tend to be Jewish while gentiles congregate on other streets. This is strikingly evident during the Christmas season when outdoor decorations are not evenly distributed throughout the suburb but appear on clusters of houses.

Jewish wealth is relatively new and obviously displayed. Much of the anti-semitism of the thirties sprang from the growth of certain Jewish enterprises in the retail field, particularly in groceries, where Steinberg supermarkets were invading areas previously served by French-Canadian corner groceries. At every turn, French Canadians encountered signs of Jewish business progress. At the same time, prosperous Jews showed a voracious appetite for status symbols that was closer to the French-Canadian than the Anglo-Saxon taste. They bought expensive cars and clothes, ate in the best restaurants, and stuffed their new homes with the latest furniture. In fact, they did all the things that the average French

Canadian would have done if he had only acquired the means to indulge his whims. The French Canadian found this even more upsetting than the vast but remote wealth of the sedate Westmounters.

The Jewish community in Montreal also carries within it a living symbol of wealth, Samuel Bronfman, who is one of the richest if not *the* richest man in Canada. In the course of "Mr Sam's" lifetime, Bronfman interests have grown from a mail-order liquor business in Winnipeg to an international empire containing among other things distilleries, wineries, skyscrapers, supermarkets, bowling alleys, and a genuine baroness (Samuel Bronfman's daughter, Minda, the Baroness Alain de Gunzburg).

Highly organized charities — the English terms "charity" and "righteousness" are significantly expressed in a single Hebrew word, "tzadakh" — have all but eliminated pockets of poverty within the Jewish community. There has not been a Jewish orphanage in Montreal since the end of World War II. Corporate and family contributions by the Bronfmans to the annual joint Jewish campaign, for example, are said to amount to something approaching half a million dollars a year.

Another indication of the community's relative wealth can be gained from the province's baffling system of tax-supported confessional schools. For school taxation (if not social) purposes, Jews in Montreal are considered to be Protestants. It has been estimated that the education of a Jewish child costs the Protestant system about $450 a year but that each Jewish child brings with him into the system about $600 a year in taxes. In this way, the Jewish taxpayers are actually "subsidizing" the schools of the English-speaking Protestant community.

Traditional Jewish respect for learning and a relatively unobstructed road to success in the professions have produced a disproportionate number of Jewish lawyers, many doctors and university professors, and a Jewish rôle in culture out of all proportion to the community's size within the English-speaking population.

English-language poetry in Quebec is dominated by such men as Irving Layton and Leonard Cohen. Many of the first chairs in the Montreal Symphony Orchestra are occupied by

Jews. There is a small number of good Jewish sculptors. Members of the community are quite active in radio and television and there are Jewish journalists, a small number, on both English and French daily newspapers in Montreal. What little there is of English-language theatre in Montreal would be impossible without Jewish talent and patronage. Cultural organizations such as the Montreal Museum of Fine Arts are benefiting more and more from Jewish generosity which in the past had a tendency to confine itself to the Jewish community.

The Jewish community has a natural aversion to being singled out as a wealthy group. Jews are quick to point out that wealth does not necessarily mean financial power, particularly when the main financial institutions in Quebec are in the hands of other groups.

"We occupy a secondary position because most of us were comparative late-comers to the city," explained a prominent Jewish businessman. "We immigrated in the late nineteenth or early twentieth centuries. By then most of the important posts were taken up by Anglo-Saxons and we were not invited to associate ourselves with those in control.

"We also were affected by the historical tendency to isolate a minority group. This isn't necessarily anti-semitism. It's just factual. The social life of the Anglo-Saxon is still tied up with his church and his club life and of course we're excluded from both. Although the success of certain Jews has brought them into close business association with well-to-do Anglo-Saxons, it remains true that sunset brings about a break."

A small group of prominent Jews recently visited Cardinal Léger in Montreal to discuss the work of the Vatican Council, particularly its formulation of a new Roman Catholic attitude toward the historical position of the Jewish race. There is no record of the informal discussion, of course, but a number of the Cardinal's Jewish visitors have said privately that they were disappointed by the Cardinal's interpretation of their own place in the Quebec community. Said one who was at the meeting, "We were struck by the Cardinal's breaking down of Quebec society into three worlds. He talked about the Anglo-Saxons, who own all the big business, banks, financial houses, and so forth. Then he talked about the Jews, who own the retail trade, despite our objections that the large department stores and most of the supermarket chains are not owned by Jews. And finally he talked about the French Canadians as the group that the other two prey on.

"This break-down was far too simple for our liking. It is true that on a per capita basis the Jewish group is wealthier than the French Canadian but there are also many Jewish clerks, taxi-drivers, and small merchants."

Claude Ryan, a relatively new and unusually sound voice in French-Canadian journalism, went to the heart of this attitude in an editorial which appeared in his newspaper, *Le Devoir*, in August, 1964.

There is in the nationalist movement at the moment a real risk of confusion between social and national problems. Because of the predominance of the English-speaking element in business and industry, it is easy and natural for us to treat in "national" terms problems which are basically social.

We speak for example of "the English" to describe bankers, industrialists, financiers and those who control our economic life. We also speak of "the Jews" to describe certain Jews who have achieved a greater success than most of their compatriots.

This manner of speaking is explained and justified by our ever-present recollection of long-standing domination. But it is far too simple a way to describe the reality. Among the Jews and the English-speaking Quebeckers there exist thousands of small wage-earners, without influence or connections, whose future scarcely differs from that of the majority of French Canadians. Contrary to what we are inclined to believe, the fate of these people does not interest the majority of important English-speaking people any more than the fate of our masses disturbs our few French-Canadian capitalists.

If we want at all costs to make our problems first and always "national," we will unjustly overlook these elements which ought to be associated completely with any authentic movement of social liberation. We will betray right at the start our proclaimed objectives.

This is a radical doctrine in French Canada — that one can

divorce any French-Canadian problem from nationalism; that one should strive to improve the lot of all Quebeckers rather than giving priority to the French-Canadian group; in other words, that there are certain social objectives which should not be discussed in the context of race and religion. French Canada is a long way from realizing this ideal.

Right now, the Jewish group feels extremely vulnerable. On one hand, they have a considerable interest in maintaining the status quo which now gives them a good share of the province's wealth. In this sense, they are on the "English" side. On the other hand, they feel a certain natural sympathy for the "underdog" French Canadians. "Twenty-five years ago," said a Jewish businessman, "we and the French Canadians were in the same boat as far as acceptance by the ruling Anglo-Saxon business group was concerned."

But their main apprehension stems from the fact that in Quebec they are powerless. They have money but not the kind of financial power that can break a political party. Unlike the Jews in the United States, they are not numerous enough to have political influence. Their future in Quebec depends on the French and English.

When he talks about the quiet revolution, almost every Jew sooner or later will say something like this: "Whenever there's trouble, the Jews suffer." Added a prominent Jewish lawyer, "But don't forget that we're no longer scared immigrants. We can't be shoved aside all that easily."

On the whole, the Jewish community in Quebec prefers to be silent while the English and French work out their problems. It feels that it cannot say anything without offending one side or the other. And it desperately wants to avoid giving offence.

A minor example.

Recently a member of one of Montreal's wealthiest Jewish families installed a trampoline in the backyard of his Westmount home. In no time at all, Anglo-Saxon children were tumbling all over the yard. With visions of damage suits dancing in his head, and anxious to get a bit of exercise himself, he mulled over the problem of removing the neighbours' children. An Anglocrat probably would have nailed up a "No

Trespassing" sign, but the Jewish Westmounter shrank from anything so direct. Finally he summoned his firm's advertising agency, one of Canada's largest, to design a tactful sign.

The agency put its best creative minds on the project. And a short time later, a discreet sign appeared beside the trampoline: "For Use by Professionals Only."

No more trespassers. No offence.

6

✤

The Capital

Any attempt to understand the new Quebec requires an effort to absorb one fact: Quebec City is not Montreal.

Elementary — but rarely appreciated by English-speaking Quebec and ignored totally by most Canadians in other provinces. Quebec City is separated from Montreal by 164 miles and a gulf of different traditions and contemporary experiences. It is no more like Montreal than Ottawa is like Toronto.

In the quiet revolution, particularly when it is not so quiet, most of the noise comes from Montreal, most of the action from Quebec City. This confuses outsiders who think of both as emanating from a single source — something identified only as "Quebec." It is particularly confusing when the noise does not seem to match the action — when students in Montreal are howling for the hides of railway and airline presidents at the same time that Premier Jean Lesage in Quebec City is talking in slow and seigniorial tones about co-operative federalism.

It has to be remembered that Quebec City remains the seat of government in the province. It is a gross error to assume, as do a certain number of Montrealers, that all the brains, spirit, and guts of the quiet revolution are in their clamorous metropolis.

When Montreal was still a trading-post looking nervously over its shoulder for stray Iroquois, Quebec City was a true colonial capital. It was the first point of significant French settlement in North America, a centre of administration and official corruption, a showpiece of French culture amid the snow and savages. When the Swedish naturalist Peter Kalm visited New France in 1749, among the flora and fauna he inspected were the ladies of the colony. With admirable scientific detachment he divided them into three categories.

The first group was composed of imports from France, the genuine article, said by Mr Kalm to "possess the politeness of the French nation." In the second group were the ladies of Quebec City, "equal to the French ladies in good breeding, having the advantage of frequently conversing with French gentlemen and ladies." Montreal women were relegated to class three and accused of "partaking too much of the pride of the Indians and of being much wanting in French good manners."

Despite Montreal's present position as the undisputed commercial and cultural centre of Quebec, the old capital retains a great deal of its original breeding. The Grande Allée set remains one of the most exclusive in Canada. French Canadians who emigrate from Montreal to Quebec City describe the *haut monde* there as a "closed society" and profess to despise it as decadent.

At the same time, with a population of only 331,000, the capital has many characteristics of a small town. More people seem to know more people. And every evening, along the Rue St Jean, there is a "paseo" in the classic Latin tradition. Groups of young men and women stroll in front of restaurants and movie theatres, eying each other, stopping, turning, and occasionally blending.

The paseo is semi-motorized. Young bloods park their open convertibles by the sidewalk and wait with spider-like patience for their chrome webs to entangle butterflies. There is a Latin beat in the air, the kind of excitement that you find only in countries where the Roman Catholic Church has attempted to inoculate a hot-blooded people with the conflicting serums of chastity and fertility. It is a magical mixture that provides more kicks than Kinsey ever dreamed of.

Night after night, the girls parade in the footsteps of their seventeenth-century ancestors. They are still the prettiest girls in Canada. It is an inexplicable thing. Some connoisseurs think that the steep streets produce a good carriage. But more likely it is a product of the hauteur and grace of the old city with its cliffs, its château of a hotel that should be horrible but is not, its narrow streets, its old churches and fine restaurants. Twenty miles from Quebec in all directions this feminine mystique peters out into homespun healthiness. Strange.

Inundated by tourists every summer, Quebec City rides the flood without a quiver. It absorbs nothing from the visitors. The French core remains uncontaminated. Outnumbering the native English-speaking residents by more than twenty-two to one, the French Canadians in Quebec City are not nearly as allergic to the English as are their cousins in Montreal. It is almost a hundred years since the English tide of settlement in the capital reached its peak and began to recede. There is no place in Quebec City today where the French Canadian does not feel at home.

The opposite is true in Montreal. There a French Canadian crashes against the "English fact" at every turn. In Quebec City there is one English-language television station and one English-language daily newspaper — the latter so removed from its environment that its linotype machines have no French accents and therefore are unable to spell many French surnames correctly. In Montreal there are two English-language daily newspapers, the larger having approximately four-fifths the circulation of the largest French-language daily, and two local English-language television stations in addition to American stations available to those with outside antennas or cable reception. Business usually is conducted in French in Quebec City. In Montreal, the more important the business discussion, the more likely it is to be in English.

Said a young priest from Quebec City who first saw Montreal as a student: "I was astounded wherever I went to hear French Canadians speaking English, badly. Of course I had heard tourists speaking English at home, but it was the first time that I had heard a lot of bad French-Canadian English."

Compared with his cousin in Quebec City, the French-Canadian Montrealer feels threatened and oppressed by the English-speaking people. This makes him more aggressive, less tolerant. The obvious competition between the two groups in Montreal has had the same effect on the English. When they have offered violence to French Canadians, it has usually been in Montreal.

It is a curious fact that English-speaking Montrealers are less hesitant about trying out their halting French in Quebec City, partly because it is often essential in dealing with unilingual French Canadians there, but also because the response is courteous and helpful, a little as if one was in a foreign country. In Montreal, the usual response is an immediate switch to English, often with ill-concealed irritation.

"Montreal is like Paris, the metropolis," said a young French-Canadian Montrealer working in Quebec City.

"In Montreal, the evolution of ideas is faster, the social restraints less noticeable than in any other part of the province. Quebec City has the social climate of a small town. A newcomer, even a French Canadian, has difficulty getting into their way of thinking.

"Not that I want to," he added before continuing: "Their society doesn't change. It creates and encourages mediocrity. They're afraid of competition from Montrealers, or anyone else from outside. I have a friend in the professions who attempted to inject some new methods into his field in Quebec City. The older members of the profession tried to drag him down."

The native view of Quebec City, on the other hand, emphasizes the stability and depth of life there compared with the shallowness and hurry-hurry atmosphere of Montreal.

"The University of Montreal is too taken up with immediate problems," sniffed a professor from Laval University in Quebec City. "The people there don't have time to think."

And an eminent if not always popular professor at the University of Montreal has been quoted as saying, in reference to his own colleagues, "The trouble with this university is that its professors insist on publishing their work as letters to the editor."

Comparisons between the two universities highlight the differences separating their cities.

Laval was founded only in 1852, more than twenty years after the official opening of McGill College, but it sprang from the old and wealthy Seminary of Quebec. Under the

French régime, the seminary had received large grants of real estate in Quebec City and the surrounding countryside, part of which it still retains. Revenue from this land enabled the priests of the seminary to start the university and retain control of it. Not so many years ago, according to legend, Laval professors wishing to travel to academic meetings sometimes had to wait for French-Canadian farmers to drop by the seminary with their rents. The priest in charge of the seminary's treasury would then dole out a travel allowance from the cabbage money.

Some time after it received its original charter from Queen Victoria, Laval was granted a second charter from Rome as a pontifical university. To this day, the Superior of the seminary is automatically Rector of Laval and the university's Royal Visitor is the Archbishop of Quebec.

The University of Montreal, which started life as a branch of Laval, also has two charters, one from the Quebec Legislative Assembly and the other from Rome. But since its official separation from Laval in 1920, it has had no richly endowed seminary to lean on. It is governed, under an extremely complex system now being revised, by a twelve-member Board of Governors appointed by the Archbishop of Montreal and by sitting governors.

Ecclesiastical power is evident in the formal structure of the University of Montreal. The Archbishop of Montreal (Cardinal Léger) is automatically Chancellor of the university. The Rector is appointed by the Vatican. He does not have to be a priest, but so far the Vatican, guided by local authorities, has preferred to select a man not only of culture but also of the cloth. However, it is expected that the next rector will be a layman.

The Church retains the right to appoint professors in the faculties of theology and philosophy. A "council of vigilance" composed of the four bishops of the ecclesiastical province of Montreal has full authority at the university on matters of faith and morals. Although this authority has rarely if ever been used, it means that in principle there is no guarantee of academic freedom.

The structure of both universities might indicate that they

are controlled in equal measure by the Church. But in Quebec, money talks with as much authority as in any other part of Canada. Its financial support of Laval gave the Church far more authority there than it enjoyed in practice at the University of Montreal, which has been from the beginning almost totally dependent on the provincial government for funds.

Anywhere else in the world, this situation would lead one to expect clerical sterility at Laval and intellectual freedom at the University of Montreal. The opposite was true during the forties and fifties. The late Premier Maurice Duplessis, who was so fond of liberty that he appropriated most of the Four Freedoms to himself exclusively, was able to keep the University of Montreal under his thumb. No obedience — no cash. But at Laval the good fathers, with a certain amount of financial independence, were able to thumb their noses at Duplessis, in moderation.

Thus there appeared at Laval during the dark Duplessis ages a lively school of social sciences under Father Georges-Henri Lévesque, a Dominican priest with a keen intellect and belief in liberal democracy. The school became one of the most important centres of resistance to Duplessis' authoritarianism at a time when the University of Montreal was refusing to hire competent and much-needed French-Canadian professors because they had been "tainted" with socialism while studying at such institutions as the London School of Economics. At the same time, Laval was creating in its faculty and student body a new generation of competent intellectuals who would be ready to move into positions of control in government and the civil service as soon as the Duplessis machine ground to a halt.

"They started to group there in the late 1930's and became influential a few years after the war," recalled a professor with good contacts at both universities.

"At that time, the University of Montreal always needed money so badly that it was in no position to resist Duplessis. The people at Laval could, to a certain extent.

"The 1949 strike at Asbestos, Quebec, when the provincial government sent its police into the area to deal with the strikers, was the turning-point. The Lévesque group at Laval supported the workers and that was the beginning of the end for Duplessis. The movement at Laval reached its peak in the last ten years of the Duplessis reign but it really began about ten years before that."

"In the old days," said a French-speaking Montreal newspaper editor, "opposition to Duplessis was centred in the universities and in the labour field.

"The university people were the only ones who had the resources to back them up. They had the kind of research apparatus that the labour people could use. In a way, the labour unions acted as the arms of the university professors. Laval was far more independent and active in this way than the University of Montreal."

Laval lost this special role on September 7, 1959, a memorable date in the twentieth-century history of Quebec, the date of Duplessis' death. In the five years since then, the University of Montreal has grown in importance as a centre of intellectual leadership in the province. How important its influence is today, and whether it is being exerted in the right direction, is a disputed question.

This is the interpretation of events given by a professor at the University of Montreal:

"When Duplessis died, the struggle at Laval was finished. Father Lévesque, who had organized the school of social sciences in 1938, left in the early 1960's to help start the University of Butare in the new African Republic of Rwanda. Maurice Lamontagne (now Secretary of State in the Pearson government) left the faculty to enter federal politics. Others went into politics and the Quebec civil service.

"The centre of liberal thought abruptly shifted to the University of Montreal. In less than no time, the faculty in Montreal became extremely liberal. The university expanded rapidly and many young professors were hired. Then came the fight against the Jesuits, who were trying to get university charters for Collège Ste Marie and Loyola College and the professors at the University of Montreal led the fight. They became aware of themselves for the first time as a social force. They became more and more radical.

"It has reached the point where, today, no one is surprised by anything at the University of Montreal. The revolution reached a culmination in the spring of 1964 with the founding of the new magazine *Socialisme '64*, influenced strongly by members of the university's department of philosophy. The university supplied many of the leading members of Le Mouvement Laïque."

Le Mouvement Laïque is an organization supporting the establishment of non-denominational secular schools in Quebec. It is based in Montreal. In Quebec City, being in favour of Le Mouvement Laïque is worse than being in favour of nudism.

"At the same time," continued the University of Montreal professor, "our students became more dynamic and progressive. Today we have the most dynamic student body in Canada with great freedom of expression and tremendous influence. At the university today, although there is a semi-ecclesiastical set-up at the top, there is no censorship. There is a free flow of ideas."

The student body became so dynamic that it effectively closed the university for a day-long strike during the 1963-64 term, not the first students' strike which the university had experienced. During it, students erected barriers across all roads entering the campus. Only those with passes signed by student authorities were permitted to enter. There was little criticism of the strike from the older generation in French Canada although a French Canadian teaching at McGill University called it a "fascist exercise."

"Few people seemed to realize or care that the students, acting unilaterally, had succeeded in stopping the pursuit of truth," he said. "Even if it only lasted one day, it was a serious matter."

Active separatist cells sprang up at the university. Student quarters were searched by police and students detained for questioning at the height of the terrorist scares in 1963 and 1964. A small number of students and former students actually were involved in the terrorist groups. If this worried their professors, they managed to conceal it with an air of true scholastic detachment.

"There are many kinds of separatists," said one professor at the University of Montreal.

"There are the *Parti Pris* types [a small magazine launched in 1964 and steering perilously close to outright advocation of violence] and the FLQ types, or whatever other initials they use. There are others who try to reconcile certain values with separatism. In between are people like Marcel Chaput [former leader of one of the larger separatist groups in the province] who have no system at all.

"Admittedly there is some danger that young people are apt to fall into the first category and forget everything for the benefit of nationalism.

"We professors at the university were not surprised to find some violence cropping up. It was regrettable but you couldn't turn the clock back on account of it. And the violence came so suddenly and unexpectedly. If we had been able ten years ago to predict it, we certainly would have emphasized the democratic values more strongly. But we had been used to seeing the students so passive.

"I suppose that certain professors now have realized the danger. But some others might say that violence is a necessary part of the process.

"As for the students, it has to be admitted that not all of them are as strongly against violence as they should be."

This professor claimed that Laval is now considered to be "conservative, moderate — a little away from the mainstream in Quebec, which is arch-nationalism, secularism, and socialism."

In 1964 the strength of this mainstream in the University of Montreal was beginning to concern some of the French Canadians who had helped to create it. It is probably true that, at any given time in the previous three years, a majority of the students there were not separatists in the strictest sense of the word. But the separatist element included many of the most active students and was strong enough to colour the whole mass. The student newspaper, *Le Quartier Latin*, became the house organ of this activist group.

"The University of Montreal, by becoming a separatist foyer, is running the risk of putting itself out of business," said the editor of a Montreal French-language daily newspaper.

"A number of professors have been carried away by their sympathies for their students. They have begun to reason in terms of emotion.

"It is absolutely essential that our universities develop the kind of teaching that a modern state needs. A nationalist university which puts nationalist values ahead of all others is not a true university. University teaching should be valid for everyone, everywhere."

The uncertainty which surrounds the separatist movement in Quebec creates legitimate doubt as to whether the University of Montreal really is riding the wave of the future on its present course. Certainly it has been a focal point of "archnationalism, secularism, and socialism," but whether these are the doctrines of the future and whether they even form an indivisible trio is open to question. In terms of public attention, the University of Montreal has cast Laval into the shade in recent years as troubles in Montreal have overshadowed the solid achievements of the government in Quebec City, but this is a cheap achievement.

Laval continues to regard the antics in its former Montreal branch office as slightly degrading.

"The centre of dynamism has not shifted to the University of Montreal," said a former Laval professor now in the Quebec civil service. "It has shifted from Laval to the government."

7

❧

The Politicians

"Eight years ago," recalled the Anglocrat businessman, "a French-Canadian politician said something to me that was prophetic.

"'When the French Canadians in Quebec realize that they have almost unlimited power through their government,' he warned me, 'you're going to be in for a terrible period.'"

This fact suffers from no lack of appreciation today. It has become dogma in Quebec that the future of French Canada rests in the hands of the Quebec government, whether or not this government remains within Confederation. The government is seen as the only important institution in Quebec absolutely controlled by French Canadians.

The most important financial and economic institutions are in the hands of others. The national government in Ottawa is dominated by the country's English-speaking majority and, for this reason, regarded with suspicion in Quebec. What is left to the Quebecker but to use the power of the provincial government to its fullest extent?

The English-speaking Canadian can ask another question: "Hasn't this always been true? Haven't the French Canadians in Quebec always had this power at their disposal?"

"I use this argument myself when I'm talking to separatists," said the editor of a French-language Montreal newspaper, "but I resent having it given to me by English-speaking Canadians as an absolute argument. In theory we have always had this power. But the fact is that we were placed in a historical situation that produced certain results."

Under Duplessis, the provincial government expressed the fear of French Canadians. The province was in a process of rapid evolution. Industrial development was drawing people from the farms to the cities, chiefly to Montreal. Old village values no longer were adequate. French-Canadian family life, while still vigorous, was cracking under the strain. Intellectuals were beginning to question the basic tenets of Quebec education. Others were starting to wonder if Duplessis' great contribution to twentieth-century political thought — Socialism Equals Communism — was really the ultimate philosophy. Beneath the surface of Quebec during the Duplessis era, doubt was growing with cancerous rapidity.

The response of the provincial government was largely defensive. To be fair, there were positive efforts in certain fields. Technical education was vastly improved. Roads were built, albeit on expensive beds of political patronage. Industry was encouraged. Good technical services were provided to important natural resource industries such as pulp and paper. But none of this overshadowed the government's basically negative approach to change.

The philosophy seemed to be this: Changes are threats. But we cannot stop the changes. Therefore we will use them to bolster the defence of Religion, Language, and Nation. The best defence is the Union Nationale party. Therefore, Quebec will be saved if changes benefit the party.

"Capitalists always try to exert their influence on any government," explained a former member of the Duplessis cabinet. "The philosophy of our government was a philosophy of private initiative. Duplessis had a strong personal belief in private initiative and no doubt the free-enterprise group supported these views."

"Duplessis used the Anglo-Saxons to keep himself in power," said an Anglocrat in Montreal. "The English-speaking businessmen in the province are wallowing in hypocrisy now, but they were the guys who played ball."

Another Anglocrat said, "It was the French who voted for Duplessis. They have only themselves to blame."

Said a French-Canadian politician in Ottawa, borrowing a

phrase from South American politics, "Duplessis was the father of the poor and the mother of the rich.

"He used everyone for his own benefit. At times his interests seemed to coincide with the interests of English-speaking capitalists. They did nothing to help the people of the province rid themselves of Duplessis.

"In Quebec there was only a collection of individual groups all trying to play one against the other. And the Quebec government was crippled by having a lousy civil service. Up until 1957, the federal government was the undisputed master of the country."

It is futile to review the Duplessis years today in an effort to portion out responsibility. Dark as they were, they did see the first successful organized attempts by the Liberals to establish a political party in the province which consciously would reflect the will of the people.

In the 1950's, among those who were opposed to Duplessis, there emerged a new concept of politics which can be called, to use a word much in vogue in Quebec City at the moment, "creative." In the North American context, there was nothing very new about it. It was simply a method to determine both the needs and aspirations of Quebeckers, synthesize them in a political program, use this program to win an election, and then attempt to direct the province toward certain goals.

For many North American political parties, this process seems as natural as breathing. But French Canadians in Quebec had been holding their breath for two hundred years. They had been using the apparatus of democracy bestowed upon them by the conquering British but refusing to inhale its spirit. The result was governments which embodied all the worst aspects of democratic leadership — corruption, retention of power at any cost, and, most damaging of all, abandonment of the obligation to lead in favour of a slavish following of events, drifting with the current of history, scavenging bits of political and financial advantage.

The new policy was creative because it realized the potential of the Quebec government as a prime mover in the province, a centre of influence which could be nourished by an intelligent appreciation of Quebec's needs and which could devise methods to satisfy these needs. It conceived of government as a dominant rather than a parasitical element.

Not all the people working toward this ideal were official Liberals. Men such as Maurice Sauvé, now federal Minister of Forestry, and Claude Morin, Quebec's Deputy Minister of Federal-Provincial Affairs, came from an early attachment to socialism. But they realized in the fifties that the only road to political power in Quebec at that time lay through one or other of the traditional parties.

The rapid rise and fall of radical parties in Quebec, from the Bloc Populaire of World War II to the current Ralliement des Créditistes, has illustrated the strong attachment of Quebec voters to their two-party system of Rouges and Bleus. This fact, incidentally, has not been ignored by politicians who have flirted in the past three years with thoughts of leading separatist parties.

Reorganizing the Liberal party in Quebec was a slow process. In the early fifties, it was no more democratic than the Union Nationale. It had no annual convention, no proper grass-roots organization, and no intellectual wing to generate ideas. New leaders were crowned by departing leaders behind a façade of democratic election.

But if the job appeared long, there was every indication that there would be plenty of time to complete it. It looked then as if Duplessis would be in office for eternity, at the very least.

When Georges-Emile Lapalme, who resigned in mid-1964 as the province's Minister of Cultural Affairs, became Quebec Liberal Leader in 1950, he undertook to form a properly structured party. In the fall of 1955, the founding convention of the Quebec Liberal Federation was held in Montreal. The late Jean-Marie Nadeau, a Montreal lawyer and one of the leading intellectual exponents of reform in the party, was named president of the federation's political commission. But an election was called in 1956 before more than a patchwork program could be assembled and the Liberals actually lost ground to the Union Nationale.

The next few years were taken up largely by a movement to ease Lapalme from the leadership. At a leadership convention in 1958, Jean Lesage took on what still appeared to be the impossible task of defeating Duplessis.

At this critical stage, Duplessis died. He was replaced by an even more formidable opponent — Paul Sauvé, a progressive member of the Duplessis cabinet who promised for a short time to do an inside stable-cleaning job on the Union Nationale. In addition to his political and administrative ability, Sauvé was a born "seigneur" who wore leadership as if it were tailored for him. He was in office a brief 114 days before he died on January 2, 1959.

His place was taken by Antonio Barrette, one of the few veterans of the Duplessis cabinet with a reasonably clean political reputation. Unfortunately for his party, Barrette turned out to be politically naive, awkward in leadership, and without the political "presence" or skill to direct his own party effectively, let alone the province.

"If Sauvé had lived, things wouldn't have moved nearly as fast in Quebec," said a prominent Quebec Liberal.

"The Union Nationale would have remained in power. Sauvé would have changed it slowly into a Conservative party. There wouldn't have been the missionary zeal that possessed the government when the Liberals moved into office.

"Sauvé wouldn't have stood for separatist nonsense. He would have used a certain amount of quiet pressure to keep the hotheads out of the universities."

Political events in Quebec in 1959 and 1960 illustrated the influence still wielded by individual politicians even in this age of mass democracy. Millions of words have been written since then to explain the underlying factors of the Quebec revolution — the growth of a large French-Canadian urban class, economic discontent, the infection of new-nation nationalism from overseas, De Gaullism, and so forth. But the revolution would not have occurred when it did, and as it did, if the hand of fate had not plucked away Duplessis and Sauvé at that time and brought together a potent combination of men within the Quebec Liberal Federation.

The Liberal group did not really start to jell until the year before the 1960 election. Paul Gérin-Lajoie, now Quebec's first Minister of Education, had been an unsuccessful Liberal candidate in 1956 and Jean Lesage had been named party leader in 1958, but René Lévesque, Minister of Natural Resources, was brought into the party only a short while before the 1960 election. It was also about this time that a number of potential civil servants became involved in the party, university men such as Claude Morin, who were asked to help draft sections of the Liberal program. Dozens of experts in various fields were canvassed for suggestions, a process that put the party into contact with most of the French-Canadian intelligentsia, particularly those interested in social conditions. At the same time, the party's weekly newspaper, *La Réforme*, was increasing its circulation from five to forty-five thousand copies, at first under the editorship of Jean-Louis Gagnon, now a member of the Royal Commission on Bilingualism and Biculturalism, and later under the guidance of his brother, Guy Gagnon, now executive secretary to Premier Lesage.

The first large-scale scientific surveys of public opinion ever sponsored by a political party in Quebec were used by the Liberals as a guide in drawing up their program.

Local organizations were formed in all constituencies. Within the federation, committees studied political problems, federal-provincial affairs, public relations, and other areas of party activity. Annual conventions were organized at which, after the Liberal victory in 1960, the government was expected to report to the party and listen to suggestions for new activity. At each convention the Premier faced an "inquisition" behind closed doors before several hundred members of the federation's general council. Duplessis would have had apoplexy if anyone had suggested this procedure to him.

The growth of democracy within the Liberal party reflected the new appreciation of democratic freedom and action which emerged in Quebec during the final years of the Duplessis régime. For the first time a significant number of French Canadians in Quebec were attempting to use the machinery inherited from the British as an accepted vehicle for social criticism and reform.

"I am sure that the French Canadians have believed in democracy only for the past ten years or so," said one of the men associated with the movement in the fifties.

"Before, there were so many problems that were taboo for public discussion. Problems were being dealt with in the corridors of the Legislative Assembly, not in the House. I remember in 1953 meeting Jean Marchand [now president of the Confederation of National Trade Unions] and Arthur Tremblay [now Quebec's Deputy Minister of Education] and a few others in Montreal to discuss whether education could even be treated as an issue in the next provincial election."

This man, in his forties today, continued, "My generation of French Canadians started a general reassessment. For the first time, self-criticism was used.

"When I was a teen-ager, a social scientist from Ontario would come to do a study of, for instance, welfare or orphanages or the status of women. Sometimes his criticism would be quite valid but it would always be rejected. The press would leap to the defence. We were so busy defending that we never had time to examine ourselves. In the postwar period, we gained self-confidence enough to start a reappraisal."

"It is now essential to have a democratic base for a political party in Quebec," said a Liberal active in the party's higher echelons. "After the last federal election we had a meeting of the organizers who had worked during the campaign. Formerly this group had just taken instructions. But now they were all getting up and raising hell."

As the federation acquired the machinery of party democracy, it became more and more awkward to have it include both federal and provincial Liberals. There had been advantages to this arrangement in the 1950's and early 1960's when either the federal or the Quebec party, or both, was out of power. When the two were in office, waging the traditional war between Quebec and Ottawa, the double-bed arrangement in the Quebec Liberal Federation produced more dispute than delight. It was decided in 1964, with the reluctant agreement of the federal Liberals, to limit the federation to Quebec politics.

It required at least ten years for the reorganization of the Quebec Liberal Party to produce results in 1960. Today the Union Nationale has barely started on the same road. Although Union Nationale Leader Daniel Johnson has announced plans for a general convention late in 1964, at the time of writing the party had not held a convention since it gathered in 1961 to elect Johnson. Local organizations are still being formed — many still have no properly elected executive — and the process of collecting membership fees is just getting under way in 1964. At the top level, with the exception of two full-time organizers, the parliamentary group is in effect the party executive.

The process of finding a new ideological position for the party has not even begun. There is no intellectual activity in the Union Nationale comparable to the platform-making work that went on in the Liberal Federation before 1960.

"All the active brains are working for the government in one way or another," said a senior figure in the Union Nationale's parliamentary group.

At the moment the party is lost. It cannot go farther to the left than the Liberals without becoming socialist, an unthinkable development, and its old position on the right is politically unsalable, at the moment. For a time in 1963 Johnson seemed to be flirting with separatism, but he is far too canny a politician to lead his party into a cul-de-sac. New parties are yapping at the heels of the Union Nationale: Réal Caouette and his nationalist Quebec Créditistes; the Parti Socialiste de Québec, separated from outright separatism by a paper-thin screen of verbiage; and the Rassemblement pour l'Indépendance Nationale, an out-and-out separatist party threatening to enter a large number of candidates in the next provincial election. Left by Duplessis with a political philosophy and party organization that functioned only in a position of power, the Union Nationale has a great deal of work to do before it can offer itself as a serious alternative to the Liberals.

The government has to remember that power is no protection against political obsolescence. Many of the changes being made by the Liberals in Quebec will work to the party's destruction unless it continues to evolve. One obvious example of this is the government's decision to extend the voting franchise to the turbulent eighteen-to-twenty-one age group, creating a new body of voters that one minister described as "a sort of Frankenstein."

Progress depends in Quebec, as in all governments, on a small "action group" within the cabinet and civil service. In the cabinet, the essential nucleus is made up of Premier Lesage, Natural Resources Minister Lévesque, Education Minister Gérin-Lajoie, and Revenue Minister Kierans. Almost every politician and civil servant in Quebec City agrees that these four men form the core of the cabinet. A majority of them also will include Municipal Affairs Minister Pierre Laporte although, in some respects, he falls into a special category. Some of ex-journalist Laporte's former newspaper associates in Montreal say that he "lacks imagination." He makes no claim to be a thinking-man's politician — as do all the other action-group members to a greater or lesser extent — but he probably has more native political sense than all the others put together, with the exception of Lesage. His appointment as Government Leader in the Assembly in the summer of 1964 was a sign that Lesage might be using him to balance the rival political ambitions of Lévesque and Gérin-Lajoie.

"Laporte is strong with the parliamentary group," said a young civil servant, not a member of Laporte's department.

"He keeps in closer touch with the ordinary members than do many of the ministers. When he's doing something in a member's riding, he makes sure that the member knows all about it and gets as much credit for it as possible. Politicians don't forget that kind of thing. He's building up a lot of support for himself."

This was reflected in the summer of 1964 when a group of provincial Liberal members accompanied a delegation of French-Canadian businessmen on a tour of Hydro-Québec's massive hydro-electric developments on the Manicouagan River. One businessman who asked the politicians what would happen if Lesage died suddenly, reported later that they had all named Laporte as the successor.

Unlike Lévesque, Laporte makes no bones about being in politics to stay.

"I like it," he said in the summer of 1964, looking back on his education as a lawyer, his seventeen years as a journalist, and his thirty months in politics. "Of course I worry about what might happen if we are beaten in a few years. I would be too old to open a law office. But that isn't a real consideration. I'm extremely happy in politics."

Laporte also has good relations with Montreal's Mayor Jean Drapeau — a political ally not to be sneezed at. He is openly complimentary about Montreal's "competent, aggressive, and progressive" administration.

Many people in Quebec place Industry and Commerce Minister Gérard Lévesque among the progressives in the cabinet although he is not a member of the inner circle.

The former leader, Georges Lapalme, before he resigned from the cabinet in 1964, was an influential enigma, progressive in the sense that he was more nationalistic than many of his younger colleagues, conservative in the fact that he belonged to an older generation.

The "conservative" wing of the cabinet was weakened in the fall of 1964 when former Attorney-General René Hamel was named a judge of the Quebec Superior Court, and former Minister of Tourism, Fish, and Game Lionel Bertrand was appointed to the Legislative Council. But the new Attorney-General, Claude Wagner, a former judge with a somewhat authoritarian cast of mind, appeared to be aligning himself with the conservatives. However, this kind of classification can be misleading. A politician can be progressive in some respects, conservative in others. René Lévesque himself was accused of conservatism when he supported a "hoist" of Gérin-Lajoie's original legislation setting up the province's first education department after Catholic bishops objected to certain aspects.

"Lévesque is becoming a conservative and doesn't like it," explained a young civil servant. "That's why he feels that he has to break out now and then in radical fashion."

This statement hints at the rivalry between the two "dauphins" in the cabinet, René Lévesque and Paul Gérin-Lajoie, which further complicates the power picture inside the action group.

"Relations between the two are cool," said the same civil servant.

"Gérin-Lajoie probably has never forgiven Lévesque for taking the conservative side on the education issue," said one of the Education Minister's associates. Other people in the education department claimed that Lévesque was in cahoots with the Church on the education issue. "All I know," said one, "is that every time we went to the Cardinal's Palace in Montreal, it seemed as if Lévesque had been there the week before."

The two men often don't operate on the same wave length. After the 1960 election, Gérin-Lajoie approached Lévesque about the government's hiring policy on the Carillon Dam in Gérin-Lajoie's riding. Most of the workers on the project were said to be Union Nationale people. Some time after the 1960 election the situation remained unchanged. Lévesque was against making any wholesale changes, and this caused a certain amount of friction between the two men at the start of their careers in the cabinet. Both had valid arguments. Lévesque was against anything that even smacked of patronage while Gérin-Lajoie was faced with a situation created by patronage that was not only unfair but politically dangerous.

Gérin-Lajoie is regarded with more confidence than the mercurial Lévesque by the Anglostocracy. A former Rhodes scholar, an expert on constitutional questions, methodical even in his political showmanship — his barnstorming 1963 campaign through the province in support of his education bill was a masterpiece of applied public relations — he is the kind of Quebec politician that English-speaking Canadians feel that they can understand. An associate described him as "Oxfordian." But it would be inaccurate to say at this time that either Gérin-Lajoie or Lévesque heads a group within the cabinet. On most issues they find themselves on the same side.

"Without the presence of Lévesque and Gérin-Lajoie, the cabinet would have deteriorated within two years," said a French-Canadian newspaper editor. "The real opposition in Quebec City comes not from the Union Nationale but from the conservatives in the cabinet."

There is one member of the action group for whom the words "progressive" and "conservative" have little relevance. The Premier himself is pure politician. He has the "grandeur" that is an essential quality of political leadership in Quebec — and something that Lévesque has yet to obtain — combined with an ability to formulate policy from the political ideas of others and his instinctive assessment of popular opinion. His leadership in the cabinet has survived recurring rumours that one or another of his ministers, usually René Lévesque, is threatening to gain control. Although he has shown signs of strain at times, on the whole he has achieved a remarkable record in a time of rapid fluctuation of opinion in Quebec, maintaining his position in the cabinet, his popularity among the people (if not among the Press Gallery journalists in Quebec City), and reasonably good relations with the federal government.

"Lesage is in a class by himself," said a young civil servant. "He holds all the pieces together."

"He is good for a period of transition," said a French-Canadian editor. "Without him the whole revolution might have been brought to the breaking-point too quickly."

Lesage thrives on politics. His wife has told friends a revealing story about a visit she and her husband made to the west coast of the United States when he was a member of the federal cabinet. Lesage liked California so much that at one point his wife jokingly suggested that they should settle there.

"Find me a little town where I can 'faire la politique,'" he laughed, "and I'll do it."

All his associates agree, privately, that the Premier is not an original political thinker.

"He never had a big idea in his life," said a newspaper editor. "You can attack one of his major policies and it won't bother him in the least. But get him on some small, personal point and he'll explode."

"Lesage implements the program but on follow-ups and new policies, he never takes the lead," explained one of his closer associates in the civil service. "One reason for this is that, in Quebec, if the premier says something, it's taken as law. That's the Quebec mentality. If the premier makes a speech and says why don't we do such-and-such a thing, the next day everybody assumes that such-and-such a thing is as good as done. That's why we have a certain freedom for other cabinet members. Cabinet solidarity applies to things decided but not always to new possibilities."

"Pearson is a statesman, sometimes a politician; Lesage is a politician, sometimes a statesman," said another influential civil servant who has worked closely with the Premier. "Pearson has more personal ideas that Lesage. I imagine that Pearson is not as easy to influence. Lesage is a man of action. He has all the qualities and vices of a man of action. He thinks fast and acts fast."

The same qualities make him a poker player to be feared, according to some of his cabinet colleagues. They remember being cleaned out by the Premier at the famous fishing-camp conference at Lac à l'Epaule in September, 1962, when the main outlines of the 1962 campaign were decided. Lesage, who is said to have won about three hundred dollars in an after-hours poker game at the two-day conference, was described by one of the losers as "an aggressive player who forces the game."

"Pearson is afraid of what Lesage might do in certain circumstances," another Quebec civil servant speculated. "He is not afraid of Lesage personally but he fears the evaluation that Lesage might make of a certain situation."

In other words, Lesage has the born politician's instinct for self-preservation. In any contest between Quebec and Ottawa, he would turn on Ottawa mercilessly if it were necessary to save his own political hide. The same sobering thought cannot be far from the minds of potential rebels in the cabinet. He would be a ruthless political enemy.

And now we come to René Lévesque, who defies analysis, by others or by himself. This elusiveness has made analysing Lévesque one of the most popular cocktail-party games in Quebec. Some of its most avid players are the politicians and civil servants who work with him in Quebec City and who are, to a surprising extent, no wiser than the general public when it comes to defining the ultimate goals of the man.

"What Lévesque wants is what we all want, but he may have a way of saying it that is different," explained a young colleague in his department.

Lévesque came to politics through television journalism. Radio-Canada gave him a public image and the producers' strike there in 1959 gave him his first whiff of political warfare. After the 1960 election he appropriated nationalization of private electrical utilities as his own issue, helped to persuade first the cabinet and then the voters that it was a good idea, and after the 1962 election victory presided over the implementation of the policy as Minister of Natural Resources. He is a fast, nervous talker, a sponge for information, a mule for work, and something of a "red peril" for many English-speaking Canadians within and outside of Quebec.

"He's got imagination, and that's never forgiven a politician in Canada," said a French-Canadian editor.

"Yes, I know, sometimes he says things which are hard to explain. Sometimes I disagree with what he says, but, so far, I don't disagree with what he has done. And after all, actions speak louder than words."

Not to everyone in Canada. When Lévesque made his famous "without-violence-if-at-all-possible" speech to a group of French-Canadian college students in Montreal in the spring of 1964, newspapers of both languages fell on him like a ton of brickbats. Even when he clarified his statement in what amounted to the strongest condemnation of terrorism ever issued by a Quebec cabinet minister, at least one newspaper righteously continued to remind him to watch his tongue in future. This episode occurred shortly after *MacLean's* magazine ran a story about Lévesque's efforts to extend Quebec's jurisdiction over the Eskimos in the northern part of the province. The cover of the magazine carried a silly headline about the "territorial ambitions" of Lévesque that not only misled readers but led Lévesque himself to talk privately about a Toronto plot to discredit him in the eyes of English-speaking Canadians. To some French Canadians, it looked almost as if English-language journalists were trying to drive a wedge between Lévesque and the Lesage government, making him look as radical as possible and then giving him a choice between adopting their radical image or apologetically rejecting it.

This tactic appeared extremely dangerous to many French Canadians. Viewed from the French-Canadian side, Lévesque has often appeared to be one of the few links between the

Lesage government and a socialist-minded younger generation — a link that no one should heedlessly sever.

Of course if one believes that Lévesque is a potential separatist leader, this justifies efforts to paint him in his true colours. But he has given few grounds for this interpretation and his closest associates in Quebec all claim that he is far too pragmatic to risk cutting himself off from the mainstream of political life in Quebec by joining a separatist group whose future, even with Lévesque at the helm, looks extremely chancy in 1964.

"He refuses to be caught in formulas," said one of his advisors. "He has a rational side to his emotional approach, a strong rational side. But his difficulty is in getting things lined up, to get a sequence of priorities in his own mind."

"He'll try to get as many opinions as possible on a problem," said another civil servant. "When I advise him on a decision, I know that he's going to compare my advice with the opinions of others before making up his mind."

"All this talk about Lévesque dominating the Quebec cabinet is pure folklore," said a French-Canadian member of the federal cabinet. "Lesage isn't a man of ideas but he has the confidence of the whole cabinet.

"And I think that René realizes that he can't achieve anything in Quebec without a strong, structured party to work through. I think that he is satisfied to fight for his ideas in a traditional party with all its weaknesses. He's too much of a realist to break away."

If he did, there is no certainty about the number of Liberals who would join him. A few tests of strength inside the party have shown Lévesque that its members do not always respond to him as quickly as university students.

"Lévesque knows very little about the party as such," said one Liberal, about the same age as Lévesque but a veteran party man. "He came in only a short time before the 1960 election, after the platform was drawn up. He didn't go through the Dark Ages with us and this is one of his problems in trying to get party support for certain things that he wants.

"The same thing holds true for Eric Kierans."

A cabinet colleague explained the controversial phrases in

Lévesque's speeches by saying that the Minister of Natural Resources "still talks like a newspaperman, not like a politician."

"But he's darn good when he's dealing with other politicians," he insisted. "When he acts as a minister of the government, he is reasonable and very good. In fact, he surprises me."

A Quebec civil servant who does not work in Lévesque's department described him as "a little bit of a prima donna, a 'cabotin' [ham]. You can almost see him saying to an audience, 'Just get a load of my direct approach.' He likes to say things with his tongue in his cheek, or with his thumb to his nose. There's an Anglo-Saxon idea that French Canadians should sit in a corner and not indulge in that sort of thing. But René says, 'I don't want to be a good boy. This is the sort of thing you don't want to hear? All right, I'll say it!' "

Pragmatist, performer, intellectual-in-a-hurry, humanist, humorist — even after all Lévesque's endearing characteristics are taken into the picture, the disturbing fact remains that he is a potential trouble-maker in Quebec, a potential separatist, a potential party leader — in fact, a potential anything. The only thing that is clear in his own mind is the goal: "a strong Quebec, a growing and dynamic Quebec," as one of the men in his own department phrased it. But the road to that goal remains hidden from Lévesque. This is why he shoots all over the map in his speeches. He will pick up an idea one day and try it out on an audience (and on all the newspaper editors in the country) the next.

At a cocktail party in Quebec City, Lévesque was involved in a discussion with a journalist of the Quebec Press Gallery about some aspect of federal-provincial relations. At one point the journalist shrugged his shoulders and said, "Well, Confederation's not sacred, I suppose." Several days later the journalist was running his eyes over the headlines in his own newspaper when the same sentence caught his attention. Lévesque had informed an Ontario audience, much to their consternation, that Confederation was not sacred.

One of my few newspaper articles that have stood the test of months is a column on Lévesque which appeared in January,

1964, in the *Montreal Star* and the Southam newspapers. I am going to quote a rather long excerpt from it.

When René Lévesque is speaking, there isn't much time to think. Ideas flash like computer lights. Impromptu phrases tear through sentences like tracer bullets.

It's heady stuff to listen to, difficult to report. For a journalist, it's torture. No other politician makes a journalist more aware of the difficulties of communication, the weaknesses and dangers inherent in the so-called "straight news story."

When René Lévesque was speaking here last Monday night in the Liberals' Reform Club, I wanted to run up from the press table and muzzle him. Even as I frantically scribbled notes, I could see the headlines in many newspapers across Canada the next day. Once again Quebec's Minister of Natural Resources would rise up before the quiet people of English Canada like a fire-breathing dragon. More ultimatums. More hysterical statements about the "destiny" of Quebec.

Late that night, as I transferred his sentences to the type-written page, I knew that I was lining him up for the Ontario executioners. It wasn't fatal this time. But one of these days, Lévesque is going to crucify himself on a cross of his own words and the cross will be constructed by a journalist who knows in his heart of hearts that he is writing Lévesque's words but caricaturing his thoughts.

After a career in journalism, Lévesque must be aware of this. The trouble is, he is still too often the journalist and too seldom the politician. He is torn between the journalist's desire to say what he thinks, quickly and under pressure, trusting to instinct, and the politician's calculated reserve.

Every politician, before he utters a word, listens to the word first with an inner ear more sensitive to dangerous nuances than the ears of his worst political enemy. Either Lévesque has no inner ear, which is hard to believe, or he simply refuses to be crippled in his utterances by listening to it.

He tries honestly to say what he thinks. And he does. But only if it is taken in the context of the history of Lévesque and Quebec does it make sense and not sensationalism.

Look at him, standing in the Reform Club before an audi-

*ence of taller, fatter, richer English-speaking businessmen.
He is not just tired. He is running on pure adrenalin. The
pouches under his eyes look as if they were drawn by a National Union cartoonist. He smiles as frequently as ever but
quickly and nervously. He is so pooped that he is afraid to
relax.*

*For more than three years Lévesque has been obsessed, not
by politics but by the knowledge that this is a critical point in
the history of Quebec. If English Canada is worried about the
future, Lévesque is both terrified and elated by it. He wants
to take every Canadian, English or French or Ukrainian, and
shake him up to his own pitch of excitement.*

*Listen to him speaking at the Reform Club for 90 minutes,
without a text, chain-smoking, his voice rough with tobacco
tar and conviction.*

*"For 300 years we have been here and this is the only part
of the world where we can feel at home.*

*"A lot of other people can find their places anywhere in the
world but there's only one place that we can call home and
that's right here.*

*"Quebec is on a road on which there is hardly any way
back, a road leading very quickly to as full a measure of self-
determination as can be allowed in the world today to a small,
compact and very resistant group of people.*

*"This requires a sort of life-and-death dedication because
there is not another single spot in the world for us."*

*Lévesque is not talking about Confederation. He is talking
about survival. If Canada disappears, what does the English
Canadian lose? He trades an imperfect system of parliamentary government for another imperfect system. He gives up
British legal practices, the* CBC, *the Queen, the National Film
Board and his treasured and traditional right to consider himself warmer and more aggressive than the British, colder and
more dignified than the Americans.*

*If Quebec disappears, what does the French Canadian lose?
Everything.*

*This is the chasm that Lévesque is running away from.
But politicians can't run fast. They are weighted with responsibility, heavy administrative machinery and political consi-*

derations. They are harnessed to the creaking wooden wagon of public opinion. For a mercurial character like Lévesque, it often must seem that he is running in a nightmare, that every step ahead requires almost unbearable effort.

It is necessary to think about these things when you listen to him; and about the Lévesque behind the politician. This is not a fanatic. He can laugh at himself. He can see many sides of a question with a mind that is as multi-faceted as a fly's eye.

The headlines obscure the fact that he has also made some of the most realistic speeches in Quebec's recent history, that he appreciates the need for foreign capital and a stable political climate in Quebec, that he fights against isolationist tendencies and that he was advocating cuts in federal defence expenditure long before federal Liberals saw the light.

If there is one thing that can be said with certainty about Lévesque, it is that he reflects the uncertainty of Quebec more graphically than any other French-Canadian politician. If he seems not to know which way to turn, it is because Quebec is hesitating at the cross-roads. If he works pragmatically at a specific problem, it reflects the hopeful practicality of the new French-Canadian spirit. If he laughs at himself — a rare quality among politicians — it is because Quebeckers even in their most extreme moments retain a saving Gallic scepticism and sense of humour.

The biography of René Lévesque will reflect in one man's career the full conflict of Quebec in the sixties.

There is another Quebec politician who must be mentioned briefly at this point. He is not a member of the provincial cabinet, but his stature in the province is at least equal to any minister's, including Lesage and Lévesque. It will surprise no Montrealer if Mayor Jean Drapeau emerges in the last half of the sixties as an important figure in provincial or federal politics.

Drapeau has travelled a long way since his Bloc Populaire days when he was an ultra-nationalist, anti-conscriptionist, and highly unsuccessful candidate in federal and provincial elections. In the twenty years since then, he has matured into a politician whose honesty and capacity for work are recognized even by his enemies, of whom there are a fair number in Montreal.

Unless he comes a cropper in future years, he will rank as the greatest mayor in the history of Montreal. He alone is responsible for obtaining the 1967 World's Fair for Montreal and for dragooning and "blackmailing" federal politicians into supporting the project. It was Drapeau who finally started digging Montreal's subway when the city was already up to its ears in expensive projects required by the Fair. If he succeeds in his latest project, a campaign to amalgamate the thirty-odd municipalities on the Island of Montreal into one big city, it will not only secure his place in the history of Montreal but transform him into the leader of a "state within a state," the political head of a region containing almost half the Quebec population and more than half of its industrial wealth.

All this has not been accomplished without treading on a number of important toes. Montrealers who made a great deal of money from curious activities in the old days still resent the do-gooder who ruined the city's reputation as the brothel of Canada. His break in 1960 with the Civic Action League earned him a new group of enemies and a literary effort to demolish his prestige by a former associate, J.-Z.-Léon Patenaude, who wrote *The True Face of Jean Drapeau* in 1962. His domination of the World's Fair during its crucial first year earned him a new flock of detractors. In 1964, those who opposed his One Big City plan were picturing him as a power-mad Napoleon in horn-rimmed glasses, an image borrowed from some of the city's newspaper cartoonists.

Drapeau's inherent tendency to ride roughshod over opposition was not lessened by his record majority in the 1962 civic election which gave him a rubber-stamp council at City Hall. He is known as a man who does not easily listen to advice or criticism from underlings or associates, with the exception of Lucien Saulnier, chairman of the city's Executive Committee, with whom he has worked in harness since 1960. Saulnier seemed to realize at the beginning of their association that while Drapeau might survive without him, he could not get along without Drapeau. This was a "political philosophy" that received Drapeau's sincere endorsement. But it would not be accurate to leave an impression that Saulnier capitulated totally to his boss. He is reputed to be practically the only man left at City Hall who is not afraid to stamp hard on a Drapeau project if he thinks that it is undesirable.

Said a Montrealer who has worked with the Mayor on a number of projects, "Anything that anyone else suggests, he doesn't like. He will not give credit to anyone else."

"Drapeau has about a hundred new ideas a week," said a member of the Quebec cabinet. "If we accept one of them, he's a great man. But ninety-nine are . . ." and he opened his arms wide in a typically Gallic gesture to express something immeasurably idiotic.

He has been known to work days at a time with almost no sleep. When he was negotiating with the Diefenbaker cabinet for approval of his World's Fair project, he started a typical week at nine o'clock on a Monday morning by driving himself to Ottawa to appear before the federal cabinet. When someone expressed surprise at the absence of a chauffeur, he is reported to have said, "Well, I trust him . . . but. . . ." While he was waiting to see the cabinet, he buttonholed an official to explain his design for a new Canadian flag. It contained, as far as the official recollects, a Christian cross in the centre against a background of ten red, white, and blue stripes representing the ten provinces.

"If you looked at it quickly, it almost appeared to be a Union Jack," said the official, "but none of its elements were British. Rather ingenious, I thought."

With Diefenbaker campaigning in Vancouver, the cabinet was unable to give Drapeau a definite answer. It asked for a written brief. The Mayor drove back to Montreal in a blinding rainstorm, went immediately to his office, and started writing. World's Fair officials were telephoned in the small hours of the morning to have sections of the brief read to them for approval. At dawn, the Mayor drove himself to the airport to make certain that the brief, written in French, was placed on the plane for Vancouver. Then he put in a normal day at the office.

"I don't think he slept at all until Thursday night, after the whole deal had been announced to city council," said an associate.

In addition to his office at City Hall, he maintains another downtown office where he can work without interruption. According to a story told by a friend of his, he decided one extraordinary evening that he was simply too tired to work and that he should go to bed at ten o'clock for a good night's sleep. He woke up at three, tossed and turned for a few minutes, got out of bed, and dressed. By four o'clock he was in the office answering letters.

"He goes into certain projects in minute detail," said a member of city council. "When the city was sponsoring a banquet for the Queen Mother some years ago, he made up the menu and selected the wine. He did everything but go into the kitchen and cook it."

It was Drapeau who discovered a village in France called Montreal which produces a palatable white wine. It is now bottled under a spécial label for the municipal restaurant on St Helen's Island, where every year the Mayor entertains the city's consular corps. It is one of his favourite functions. The old nationalist fervour has been transformed into an ambition to make Montreal one of the leading cities of the world. When Drapeau talks about Montreal, he makes Diefenbaker's Vision of the North look pallid. Here is a typical sample from a speech delivered in December, 1963: "From now on, Montreal looks to the future. It is reaching by giant strides the destiny which history and geography intend for it, worthy of the high rank which it occupies in Canada and across the world."

It appears, in 1964, that there is only one thing which can prevent Drapeau from extending his political career far beyond the limits of Montreal. Said an opponent: "If the World's Fair is a success in 1967, this man is going to emerge with the most elegant political reputation in Quebec. But he won't live to see '67. No human being can work the way he does."

The smallness of the "activist" group in the Quebec cabinet and civil service sometimes frightens its members. There is a great deal of talk in Quebec City in 1964 about the forces of conservatism, talk that is not discouraged by the emergence of Goldwater in the United States. French Canadians are supposed to be a conservative breed, although this stereotype is based on the land-hugging "habitant" and has less and less application to his grandsons in urban Quebec. Still, intelligent Liberals will talk about "the political digestive system being able to take only so much social experimentation" and wonder whether Quebec is being fed too much progress too quickly.

"Patronage is creeping back to a dangerous extent," claimed a cabinet minister. "Conservatism is trying like hell to reassert itself."

"There is some talk among us about hardening of the arteries," said another Quebec minister, "but there is still too much to be done for us to become complacent.

"The farmer is at a dead end economically. He sees prosperity in other places — on television, for instance — and he gets mad. It's all very well to work on education and highways and the World's Fair, but what about potatoes? Well, they're only potatoes, you'll say, but potatoes are potatoes and our potatoes are not being sold because our quality control isn't good, and it isn't good because our farmers haven't enough money to improve it. So we import potatoes from New Brunswick and Maine. It's a vicious circle. We've got a lot of work ahead of us in rural areas.

"And labour is becoming more and more politically conscious. Our teachers are politically active even if they don't know where they're going. All this does not mean conservatism.

"It's true that when you talk about the progressive group here, you think of four men in the cabinet and maybe ten or fifteen civil servants. But if we're such a small group, why haven't we been kicked out or moved aside? Because nobody knows how many progressives there really are in Quebec. This government wouldn't be sure of its position for long if this little group departed."

"We're certainly asking ourselves: Are we followed by a majority of citizens or do we only hear the pressure groups?"

admitted another cabinet minister. "Are we giving the patient more medicine that he can absorb?

"Some of us are afraid, but personally I don't think we've reached this stage yet. The public is still pushing us. The general attitude is, 'All right, that's done. What's for tomorrow?' Newspapers, students, labour groups, they're all jumping on us. We couldn't stop moving without having the whole province on our back."

This is the way it looks to a Quebec civil servant not long out of Laval University: "This government is a bourgeois government that is socialistic by chance. It's a dynamic conservative government." But to a senior English-speaking civil servant in Ottawa, the Quebec government is "revolutionary."

"In Quebec you have the most intellectual cabinet in Canada," he said, "and the important thing is that it is, well . . . I would use the word left-wing if I wasn't afraid of being misunderstood. They want to use the power of government to make great economic changes.

"This is a different type of group than you find, or would find, in Ottawa or the other provinces. In another province, this generation would be progressive and reforming, but in Quebec it's revolutionary."

A civil servant in Quebec put it more succinctly. "For us," he said, "the federal Liberals are just a bunch of old-timers."

The government in Quebec wants to replace the old trinity of capitalist-clergyman-politician with a new structure occupied at the top by the provincial government, the only effective economic tool controlled by French Canadians. Within the context of Confederation and the free enterprise system, this is an attempt to change the pattern of power within a "nation" to an extent that legitimately can be called revolutionary. How well it has succeeded in the initial stage can be determined by looking at the machinery of government in the new Quebec and the new generation of cogs.

8

The "Mafia"

The French Canadians who are achieving the revolution are not isolated terrorists in Montreal but members of the "Mafia" in Quebec City. This is a term used occasionally — too infrequently for a journalist's liking — to describe the new wave of bright young men who invaded the civil service in the wake of Premier Lesage's 1960 election victory.

In Quebec at the moment, they are both more and less than an efficient administrative machine. They are too few in number and too new at their jobs to form a reliable institution that moves smoothly into motion whenever a cabinet minister presses a button. But these two factors also have helped to create an élite civil service group of unusual importance, a group of "creative" civil servants who play an important rôle in policy-making and set the tone of the whole revolution.

"We're doing just what we're not supposed to do, according to the traditions of the civil service," admitted one influential member of the Mafia. "We're pushing the ministers from behind all the time. And so far, so good."

"In Ottawa," recalled one of the many Mafia leaders imported from the federal civil service, "the politicians addressed themselves to an institution, and a good one. They had a lot of respect for it.

"Here the situation is more fluid. It's a matter of individual ministers having a lot of confidence in their own groups of advisors. Each of the important ministers has his own circle of new civil servants who often wield far more influence over that particular minister than would be the case in Ottawa."

There are three main reasons for this. In the first place, the government has been in a particularly creative mood since it took office in 1960. In almost every department new policies have been introduced. The process has required a tremendous amount of brain power from a relatively small number of new-generation civil servants and naturally raised them to positions of more than ordinary influence.

In the second place, some of the new civil servants were implementing policies at least partly devised by themselves. Before the 1960 election, the Liberal party picked the brains of the French-Canadian intelligentsia for platform ideas, particularly in the universities, especially in Laval University. After the election, it picked up more than a few bodies from the same group. This is particularly evident in the education department, which has become almost a test laboratory for ideas generated by its leading civil servants when they were still teaching at university.

A third reason is rooted in the structure of the élite in Quebec. It is a very tightly knit group. Everyone seems to know everyone else, by personal acquaintance, by reputation, sometimes by blood or marriage relationship. French-Canadian society has been likened accurately to an iceberg, with a clearly defined water-line between the soggy masses and the bright, glittering, and relatively tiny élite group at the top. A typical French-Canadian newspaper editor, for instance, is an old university chum of Quebec's top labour leader, a former boss of an important cabinet minister, on informal terms with almost all other members of the cabinet, a long-time acquaintance of the Leader of the Opposition, a personal friend of virtually all the important writers in French Canada, a welcome guest at the Cardinal's Palace — in fact, a list of his friends and acquaintances would amount to a comprehensive *Who's Who* for French Canada. He knows instinctively where all these people stand in the hierarchy, what their politics are, approximately how wealthy they are, how much education they have and where they received it, how religious they are, and whether or not they have mistresses in apartments on Sherbrooke Street.

When a certain department in Quebec was looking for a

man to fill an important post recently, the minister asked his senior civil servants to jot down suggested names. The same name appeared at the top of each list.

Another example: A deputy minister was looking vaguely for an assistant in the spring of 1964. Within a short time, this fact became known to a junior civil servant in another department. Through him it was transmitted to his wife who was studying at the time at the London School of Economics. She informed her husband that an excellent French-Canadian candidate for the job was about to finish his studies at the school. The junior civil servant called the deputy minister and said, "There's a genius coming back from London." He was hired sight unseen.

Ministers and civil servants form a much more unified team in Quebec than in Ottawa, where both the politicians and civil servants are drawn from different areas, social backgrounds, religions, and educational institutions. Even when two civil servants in Quebec have no family, professional, or school ties, they know a great deal about each other simply because they belong to the same remarkably homogeneous national group. In fact the Quebec civil service is a prime example of that kind of natural discrimination which has worked against the French Canadian in the business world of Montreal. An English-speaking Quebecker in the Quebec civil service is much more of an oddity than a French Canadian on St James Street. You might as well look for an Iroquois on the board of the Royal Bank of Canada.

This situation is so well understood that it almost never occurs to an English-speaking Canadian to apply for a job in the Quebec civil service.

So desperate was the province's Department of Education for a senior economist recently that it advertised the position, with an annual salary of between $14,000 and $18,000, in a number of English-language professional journals in North America and Europe. The department bent over backwards in its specifications, suggesting that a "working knowledge" of French would be "preferred" in the applicant. There was no response at all.

Of course, this one-big-family atmosphere in Quebec was

not invented by the Mafia. If anything, it was even more marked during the Duplessis régime, when the civil service was to a certain extent a pasture for political workhorses.

"Before 1960 there was no proper structure in the civil service here," claimed a young civil servant. "The civil service was very small and composed largely of Quebec City residents. When they had a problem, they simply picked up the phone and called a friend. The relationships were really folklorique." (This lovely word is practically a generic term in Quebec City for old-time politics and government administration. When a politician or civil servant is described as "folklorique" it means that he is a quaint relic of the bad old days in Quebec when French Canadians tried with spectacular lack of success to run a government as if it were a family business.)

In the old civil service family there was only one chief. This does not mean that there were not many competent technicians working for the government, particularly in the departments dealing with natural resources. But ministers, let alone their deputies, carried little weight in deciding government policy.

"We had one senior man in our department left over from the old days," explained a leading member of the Mafia.

"He was a good man when it came to executing policy. But every time a question came up, even on a small matter, he would refer the question baldly to the minister. The rest of us were referring questions with lists of possible answers, indicating our own choice, and trying to state the alternatives. But this guy had never been trained to give an opinion."

The young civil servant objected strongly to the "Mafia" label or to any attempt to talk about young and old generations in the civil service.

"Eventually we new ones got to know the old ones. Some of them were full of qualifications but, after years in the old system, had lost their drive. Others had somehow managed to survive without being intellectually crippled. Now they belong to the 'new generation,' if you want to call it that.

"It is more accurate to talk about a new spirit in the civil service. There are lots of newcomers who pay lip service to this new spirit and don't give a damn about it.

"It's true," he said, "that we're getting a better type these days, people who would never have dreamed before of applying to the provincial government for a job.

"When the department hired engineers in the old days, for instance, it didn't exactly get the dregs but many came here for the wrong reasons, because their wife or fiancée didn't want to leave Quebec City, something like that. There wasn't much positive motivation. And when they got into the department, they gave little in the way of advice or opinion. They weren't asked for it.

"The number that somehow managed to keep up their interest is a bit surprising. And after the change in government, when they were persuaded that their jobs were safe and that their opinions would be listened to — why, some of the most dynamic people in our department today are the ones who sat here for fourteen years or more and did nothing under the old régime."

Quite a few of the "old ones" are still in positions of authority — a surprising number in view of the time-honoured tradition in Quebec of purging and re-stuffing the civil service every time the government changes. In the summer of 1964, a civil servant compiled from memory a rough list of nineteen deputy ministers of whom eight were classified as survivors from the Duplessis era. Most of these were working in departments of secondary importance. With the exception of Revenue Minister Kierans, the members of the action group in the cabinet were working with new deputy ministers.

The new spirit consists in large measure of excitement, a feeling that the composition and destiny of Quebec is being altered radically, that authority is eager for new ideas, that the civil service and not the university or separatist groups is the real workshop where the future of the province is being shaped. Among the many young men in senior positions, there is the intoxication of being in charge at an age when their physical and intellectual energy is almost unlimited.

"The whole situation here is abnormal," said one. "Look at me — at thirty-five, I'm a deputy minister. In any other civilized country, I would be a department head at best. There's a feeling that this government reflects the will of the younger and middle generation."

"Admittedly, I'm earning more money here than if I had stayed in Ottawa," said another. "But the most important thing was that I was interested in what was going on in Quebec. There was more rapid advancement here, a chance to influence policy, and a lot more fun."

The new generation itself breaks down into two groups, the over-thirty veterans who came largely from university faculties, the federal civil service, and private industry, and what one might call the "Junior Mafia" recruited almost directly from university graduates.

"I felt that the only place to get something done was up here," said a member of the latter group, an ex-Montrealer.

"A lot of the work is obscure, but it's inspiring, if you feel it. You get almost dizzy sometimes, like someone caught up in a wave. You move too fast. You have no experience, but neither has anyone else.

"In France right now the young men have to sit and wait. I imagine it's the same in English Canada. But in Quebec the whole structure is changing. You don't feel compressed into a pattern. You feel that the collectivity is open to suggestion.

"This, not separatism, is the real challenge — to build this province in the way that the people want it."

Another young civil servant summed it up by saying, "There's no handbook here in Quebec."

And another, "It's sort of an apostolate."

Quebec must be the only place in North America in 1964 where the civil service seems as glamorous as the Foreign Legion, where a dynamic director-general of buildings and equipment for a department can be known as "Flash Gordon" to his contemporaries.

"I had ten close friends in my law class at the University of Montreal and not one of them is working for the big firms on St James Street," a young civil servant said proudly.

"Two are working, like myself, for the province. Another is a professor of criminal law in the Congo. One is in the labour movement. Another is working for the World's Fair. All of us are doing something useful."

This particular young man was twenty-nine years of age, a lawyer by training, a town planner by profession. Like many of his colleagues in the civil service, he based his work on the belief that Quebec is not only an exciting but a unique place and that he himself has some special contribution to make. His professional "creed" was built around a belief that it is possible to express unique aspects of the French-Canadian way of life through town planning.

"When Lesage says that Quebec is different from the other provinces, I want to know: How? In what respect?" he said. "Well, in my own field, I can see that the French Canadian is a type who likes to live collectively and that he is quite different from the Anglo-Saxon in this. You can see it in the way he used to build villages with all the houses clustered close to the road. You can see it in the taverns and corner groceries of east-end Montreal. They have social significance. East-end Montreal has a real meaning for me.

"Now the question is: How do you reflect this French-Canadian character in an urban industrial society? I dislike the modern suburb, not for the usual North American reasons but because it doesn't correspond to the French-Canadian way of life. I want to rebuild our cities according to the character of the people."

Although its recruiting program was abetted by this idealistic approach, the Lesage government discovered soon after taking office in 1960 that the layer of technical talent in French Canada was dangerously thin. The federal civil service in Ottawa and in Quebec contributed some trained men, after Quebec hiked its salaries to a competitive level, but this was a limited source of supply. Private enterprise supplied some men but took away others. Universities churned out a fairly plentiful supply of young economists and social scientists but there was and still is a critical shortage of people in the department-head category, the men between thirty-five and forty-five years of age who should have been working up through the departments during the Duplessis years. Until 1960, people with these qualifications simply weren't hired in any numbers by the province.

An assistant deputy minister claimed that seven-eighths of

his 1946 graduating class of economists at Laval University went to work outside the province. He himself had worked for the Dominion Bureau of Statistics, a supermarket chain in Montreal, and the United Nations in North Africa before entering the Quebec civil service in 1961.

"I belonged to the generation that couldn't find opportunity in Quebec, not only in English-speaking business but in our own government," he said. "There was no need for technocrats in the civil service under Duplessis. And any graduate of the school of social sciences at Laval had a black mark against him as far as the provincial government was concerned."

In the Department of Industry and Commerce, a civil servant said that the $15,000-a-year position of director of the Bureau of Statistics had been open for eighteen months and still no acceptable candidate was in sight.

"There's a terrific shortage of economists, sociologists, and demographers with five or six years' experience," he said. "We don't have any problem picking up men fresh out of university but there's no one for them to work under."

In any other province, the civil service would be able to search for candidates across North America and in the United Kingdom. Quebec's only outside sources of qualified personnel are France and Belgium, both booming in the sixties and taking full advantage of their own reserves of trained manpower. Even French imports are not always blended easily into the local mix. Although the language of the Quebec civil service is French, the methods are strictly North American. A majority of the new French-Canadian civil servants with postgraduate university training have received it in the United States and, to a lesser extent, England and France.

Despite the difficulties involved in exchanging information and personnel with European civil services, the Quebec Department of Industry and Commerce during the winter of 1963-64 had two men working and receiving instruction in the French equivalent of the Dominion Bureau of Statistics. It was hoped that four more men would be able to go from the department to Paris in the autumn of 1964. Two or three experts loaned by the French government were expected to arrive in 1965 to occupy positions requiring experienced men. They will train French-Canadian successors. Negotiations were under way for a similar arrangement with Belgium.

One result of the shortage of trained civil servants has been a severe "brain drain" from French-Canadian universities. There are quite a few former university professors in the Quebec civil service today and sometimes the professors who remained behind might as well be working for the government on a full-time basis. There has been such a dire need for technical studies in many areas that professors have done a land-office business hiring out their talents to the highest bidders. A number of professors now earn more from this "free-lance" work than from their university jobs. Estimates of total annual incomes for top French-Canadian sociologists and economists on the faculties of universities range up to $50,000.

"The former government created road contractors," said one civil servant. "This government has created contractors in research.

"Now professors won't move from universities into government service because they are making fortunes by 'moonlighting.' They use their students to help with the research and sometimes they sell virtually the same study to both the federal and provincial governments. It's a racket."

A deputy minister recalled giving a contract for a thousand-dollar study to a professor. The result was disappointing and somehow familiar. The deputy discovered that the professor had done little more than interview the people in the deputy's own department and compile a summary of their opinions.

"Many of the university professors today spend most of their time writing briefs for the government, labour unions, school boards, and other groups — often briefs of no great value," said a senior civil servant, himself a former professor.

"This bleeds the universities of their more progressive spirits. They don't have enough time left for their real jobs. A large number of professors are just dilapidating themselves.

"I have a feeling that, because of this, the universities are not giving the dynamic leadership that they gave in the fifties. Too many professors are no longer concerned with basic issues."

Some years ago, it was suggested to professors at Laval University that they should limit their outside earnings to 20 per cent of their university incomes. Surplus earnings would be used to set up a research fund at the university. The proposal was laughed out of court. When it came to making money from the government, some French-Canadian professors have shown themselves to be just as greedy and not much more scrupulous than road or bridge contractors.

A curious by-product of the personnel shortage in Quebec is the conviction among civil servants that separatism, regardless of its theoretical desirability, is simply impractical in the immediate future. The civil servant, removed from Montreal's turbulent climate, is usually far too busy with urgent problems to give much more than formal recognition to separatism as a possible, if remote, solution to Quebec's problems. When he does think of it, he thinks also of the gaps in the staff of his own department. He asks himself: What would happen if Quebec suddenly had to find men to operate the various services now administered in Quebec by the federal civil service: customs, certain police matters, subsidized housing, supervision of navigable waters, post office, fisheries, and so forth? It is true that many of these federal services in Quebec are staffed by French Canadians, but this existing personnel would not be sufficient in most cases to operate an independent service.

In the Lesage government's first years in office, everyone in Quebec was talking about Le Plan. In detail it was vague, in theory, miraculous. By having a planned economy, planned by and for French Canadians, Quebeckers at last would control their own destiny.

Le Plan was much better than Duplessis' old "autonomy" business because English-speaking Canadians couldn't possibly object to it. In practically every capital of the world in the sixties, even in Ottawa, economic planning was the slogan of the day.

No one was certain about the kind of planning that Quebec would require. "Something like the French plan," was the usual response because, in up-to-date Quebec, if it's from France it's got to be good. Moreover, the French plan was conveniently obscure. Even in France, only a few experts seemed to understand what it was all about. Frenchmen who visited Quebec to explain it immediately walked to blackboards and vanished in clouds of chalk-dust and mathematical formulae.

In February, 1961, the Quebec legislature created the Economic Advisory Council, a fifteen-member body linked to the government by having four deputy ministers and the president of Hydro-Québec as associate members. The council, in addition to being assigned a number of special projects, was ordered to start work on Le Plan. Premier Lesage stated the basic philosophy:

The citizens of Quebec do not have at their disposal large accumulations of capital. . . . Quebeckers now have only one powerful institution: their government. And now they want to use this institution to build the new era to which perhaps they could not otherwise aspire.

In his budget speech in April, 1963, the Premier announced that Plan I would be a five-year plan starting in 1965. Early in 1964 newspaper correspondents were being informed that schedules for drawing up the 1976-80 plan were already laid down.

But by the summer of 1964, the mood in Quebec had changed so abruptly that it was becoming almost impolite to inquire about Plan I. Civil servants whispered that it really should never have been mentioned in the 1963 budget speech.

"Sometimes there's too much planning and not enough dirty work on specific projects," said one of the action-group ministers.

"Lesage made a mistake when he said that the first plan would be ready by 1965. Eventually we will have a plan, but it will be like the first French plan after the wartime occupation, a simple matter of stating what is needed and where. It will be planning on a commando basis, possibly concentrating only on three or four sick areas in the economy. It will be a plan based strictly on the things that we know."

Another minister, entering a federal-provincial conference called in 1964 to discuss a resource industry, was handed two lengthy briefs prepared by the Economic Advisory Council.

He glanced through them and dumped them into the waste-paper basket as he entered the conference room. The story went along the civil service grapevine in Quebec City in a few days.

"The Economic Advisory Council isn't worth a damn," said another important minister. "They keep producing documents talking about the first phase, the second phase, and so forth. Hell, this is a free economy."

How much planning is possible in the North American economy? How much planning authority can a province exercise within Confederation when it controls neither money nor tariffs nor major economic policies? Questions such as these puncture some of the grandiose talk about Le Plan in Quebec.

More significant to date has been the growth of planning and the "planning mentality" in the civil service. Every time you turn around in Quebec City, you bump into another planning committee. Almost every department seems to have one. Ministers involved in the exploitation of natural resources sit on a "permanent ministerial planning committee." Their deputies belong to a "permanent committee on development of resources." Beneath them, bright young technocrats from the civil service sit on technical subcommittees engaged in what often amounts to short-range planning.

When a major problem crops up — hydro-electric nationalization, pensions, or creation of a steel industry — task forces are recruited within and outside of the civil service to draw up detailed plans.

The best example of this planning mentality is found today in what traditionally has been one of the most backward areas in Quebec, the Gaspé, in an organization called "Bureau d'Aménagement de l'Est du Québec Inc. (BAEQ), translated as the "Eastern Quebec Planning Bureau Inc." This is a semi-governmental organization set up officially as a private company but wholly dependent on the government for financial support. The federal and Quebec governments roughly split the cost of operating BAEQ under the Agricultural Rehabilitation and Development Act (ARDA). Created formally in July, 1963, BAEQ has as its task the economic rehabilitation of a chronically depressed region — the provincial counties of Temiscouata, Rivière-du-Loup, Rimouski, Matane, Matapédia, Gaspé North, Gaspé South, Bonaventure, and the Magdalen Islands.

About 350,000 people live in this region, many of them gaining less than a bare living from fishing, farming, logging, and casual employment. Behind the scenic beauty and rustic quaintness of the Gaspé peninsula, admired by thousands of tourists every summer, fester despair, frustration, and shiftlessness born of continual underemployment. Farmers till fields that are unable to produce a profit, a fact that can be proved scientifically by agronomists using weather records and soil tests. Fishermen use boats and techniques that make commercial failure almost a foregone conclusion. Some parts of the region are blessed with good potato-growing soil, yet there is an import of potatoes from the Maritime provinces. In some districts about 60 per cent of the population is on social assistance. One economist has estimated that about fifteen communities should be abandoned and their inhabitants moved elsewhere. Social assistance pumped into the region every year amounts to more than the value of manufactured output. This last fact finally convinced federal and provincial governments that there was no point in continuing to throw good money after bad. BAEQ was organized to take a clear look at the situation, a process that will cost up to $2 million before the first comprehensive economic development plan is finished in 1966.

It is regarded throughout the province as an important pilot project, a showcase for the new generation of planners. By the summer of 1964, BAEQ had a full-time professional staff of more than 50 people in addition to 50-odd secretarial workers and 120 university students hired for temporary work. The immigration of sociologists, geographers, demographers, agronomists, economists, and other professionals into the modern BAEQ headquarters in Mont Joli was so heavy and sudden in 1963 that it created a temporary housing shortage in the town and a slight boom in rents.

Most of these men and women — about two-thirds of them are under thirty-five years of age — could pick their jobs in Montreal or Quebec City. They came to Mont Joli because salaries were high — better than in the Quebec civil service but without some fringe benefits — but mainly because word circulated quickly in Quebec that there was some sort of "Peace Corps" operating in the Gaspé. They wanted to show that their city-bred revolution had not forgotten the outlying areas of the province.

They talk a great deal about "animation sociale" — the need to inoculate the whole population of the Gaspé with their own enthusiasm. By mid-1964, committees had been formed in 120 communities activated by nine professional organizers. These citizen-groups not only channelled information about BAEQ to local people but actively participated in surveys. BAEQ was publishing its own weekly newspaper with a circulation of about five thousand copies and making its own movie and television films to explain its work to the people.

"We want to build a structure of participation," said one of the BAEQ planners. "In many areas we have to start almost at the beginning. There is less democratic tradition at the local level here than in most parts of North America. In most of these communities there is a terrific shortage of natural leaders."

By the end of its first year BAEQ was generating a flood of revolutionary ideas. In private conversation, its professional workers talked about large-scale movements of population, reorganizing transport, credit and co-operative facilities, enlarging some farms and abandoning others, developing certain "pole" communities in natural economic zones at the expense of neighbouring towns — in short, a revolutionary interference with the existing social and economic pattern.

How many of these ideas will be practical and how many will be discarded because of political reasons or insufficient "animation sociale" are big questions. They will not be answered for at least three or four years. The important fact, however, is the manner in which BAEQ planners are tackling the job.

They may have grandiose schemes in the backs of their heads but they are trying to look at facts. The initial phase of their work is devoted to collecting as much information as possible about the region. In 1964 they were analysing 16,000 aerial photographs covering the whole region, using them to compile an inventory of geological, agricultural, forest, and other resources. Interpretation of the photographs was being spot-checked by crews on the ground. Incomes, occupations, debts, fish populations, peat moss harvests, tourist habits, soil and grass temperatures, even an "inventory" of the local clergy compiled by a priest from Laval University — every conceivable fact about the region was being collected and evaluated. All plans for economic development will spring from these facts.

The same process is under way on a smaller scale in two other regions. Development schemes in the Rouge River Valley, northwest of Montreal, and the counties of Brome and Stanstead in the Eastern Townships are being preceded by intensive inventories, in these instances prepared by "Société Technique d'Aménagement Régional" (star), a private firm working under contract for the government.

The same "facts first" mentality appears strongly in the new civil service and the action group in the cabinet. Such important policies as the nationalization of electrical utilities and the pension plan were based on extensive factual dossiers.

In the case of nationalization, this technique enabled French-Canadian politicians to bolster a politically astute move with factual reasons which English-speaking owners of private utilities treated with respect. René Lévesque, touring the province with his blackboard, smothering his audiences in statistics, was preventing nationalization from becoming a rabidly nationalistic issue based on rhetoric rather than reason.

So complete was the dossier on the pension plan that when it was presented to the federal-provincial conference in Quebec City in the spring of 1964, Newfoundland's Premier Joey Smallwood was reported to have asked wryly, "Is it possible to get into the Quebec plan?" This was a far cry from the old days when Duplessis delivered classical lectures on "autonomy" to the federal government and other provinces.

In the Quebec Department of Industry and Commerce, the personnel of the Bureau of Statistics has increased since 1960 from about 55 to more than 170 people. Quebec aims by 1965 to have its own national accounts which will provide a statistical picture of the Quebec "nation" that will be almost as complete as the overall picture presented by Ottawa's Bureau of Statistics.

This represents a radical change in the French-Canadian mentality. It is the most important aspect of the planning mania. For the first time in its history, Quebec is attempting to substitute government by reason, based on facts, for government by inspiration, based on some mystical idea of "mission." For the first time, French Canada is making an effort to see itself as it is, in cold blood. It is trying to smash the rose-coloured mirror held up for two centuries by its own politicians and clergy.

The damage done to French Canadians by the politicians and priests who soothed them with the syrup of alleged cultural and religious superiority is inestimable. Instead of nourishing the competitive spirit of their people, they sapped their real pride and vitality.

In the late 1950's, a research team at McGill University discovered that French-Canadian students in their late teens believed that English-speaking people were more intelligent, dependable, ambitious, and of better character than French-speaking people. On only two traits, religiousness and kindness, did French-Canadian students give higher marks to their own language group. This was a typical example of the unforeseen and tragic end-product of the myth of French-Canadian superiority.

There is still, even today, a tendency for French Canadians to luxuriate in flattering verbiage. The most prolific dispensers of sugar-water are the separatists, with the exception of Raymond Barbeau and a few others who at least attempt to prove their case with economic arguments. The majority of separatist writers and orators offer French Canadians nothing more than the old doctrine of superiority. A new bottle but the same old syrup. And like their predecessors, they blind the French Canadians to their real achievements and sabotage their ability to function in the world that surrounds them.

While the separatists have talked, some politicians and civil servants have started the significant revolution by abandoning the old myths and concentrating on facts. This mentality already has wrought a change in the structure of power in Quebec. For the first time, French-Canadian politicians and English-speaking businessmen are starting to talk in the same terms.

"The fishing industry is a good example," said a civil servant. "We came up with statistics showing that the retail price of fish had gone up, wages in the industry had gone up, but the prices to fishermen had lagged. We wanted to know why. We called six or seven of the big companies. 'Why not drop in and talk with us?' we said. 'Maybe our statistics are wrong. Maybe we don't know all the facts. Let's hear your side.'

"In forestry, concessions come up at regular intervals. In the old days, it was a matter of sending someone from the company to have lunch with a civil servant. Sometimes a telephone call was enough: 'Same arrangement as last year, eh?' Now we've made a few studies. We have a few ideas about the industry. We want to discuss them.

"When we first went to the big steel companies to talk about a steel industry for the province, they thought we were a bunch of kids. It was obvious. They thought that they could just pat us on the head and tell us what a nice idea it was. Then we began to produce our studies. The steel companies all of a sudden sat up and paid attention. 'No,' they said, 'you can't talk about doing it in such-and-such a way.' Objections started to come, solid objections. There was a lot of serious talk. You could feel the atmosphere changing."

"We used to have a government which never asked questions," said another civil servant. "This government specializes in the art of asking difficult questions."

"During the Duplessis era, it was quite different," a prominent figure in the pulp and paper industry admitted. "It was a matter of the Premier having the president of a company for breakfast. That was his favourite trick. Uh, not trick. . . procedure. Now it's more orderly."

"At times the pulp and paper companies will say that one of our policies will be ruinous," related a civil servant in the Department of Natural Resources. "We ask them to prove it. In some cases, maybe they can prove that we are not making the right decision. In that case, we change it. The important thing is that they know that they can argue with us on a factual basis.

"Of course the pulp and paper companies were apprehensive at first. Many things were up in the air when we came in. There were leases that hadn't been renewed officially for seven years. But they soon discovered that there was a lot of room for discussion. We weren't interested in putting anyone out of business."

"Ten years ago the big companies had a rather colonial attitude," reflected a cabinet minister. "Sure, Duplessis was proud that a lot of big businessmen danced to his tune, and up to a point, they did. But not for essential things. Take —— Company, for instance. Whenever a change of lease was being considered, all the basic documents emanated from the company side. There was never any detailed study inside the government.

"We are trying to build up as much knowledge about certain fields as the companies have. That's the only way that we can deal with them constructively. Right now, for example, we've got a team of economists at —— Company to deal with a lay-off problem. Hundreds of men are involved. That's not just the company's problem. It's also our problem. We're not saying it shouldn't happen, but it shouldn't happen unexpectedly like this. We've got to know about this industry if we're going to help.

"Another company was charging off part of the overhead of the parent company in the United States to its Quebec operation. Things like that are just an economic joke. When we have competent people in our department, the climate changes."

"I like to see our people working on specific problems, like our power nationalization program," said Natural Resources Minister Lévesque. "If nationalization had seemed ideologically good but impractical, would we have gone ahead with it? I don't think so."

"There are two ways to start planning," said a junior member of the Mafia.

"One is to draw up an overall scheme based on theory and the other is to create organisms as the need arises. There may be a certain amount of confusion involved in the second way, but out of it will come the right solutions.

"The Economic Advisory Council is trying to create things from thin air. Most of them have read about Le Plan Français, but this is not France. We have to create our own methods, build up something that suits our own reality."

The new spirit of pragmatism in Quebec has produced a government and civil service that uses the techniques and talks in the language of the twentieth century. As it becomes more deeply involved in the economic life of Quebec, it inevitably will come into contact more frequently with private interests. But this contact can be constructive if both parties are talking in the same terms. They are today, for the first time.

The same spirit of pragmatism is working a revolution, still largely hidden, in Quebec's dealings with the federal government.

9

❧

Friends and Relations — Federal-Provincial

1. A CASE IN POINT

On April 16, 1964, W. A. Wilson, the *Montreal Star's* senior correspondent in Ottawa, reported that "key Liberal personalities regard this as the most crucial week in the life of the Pearson government upon which its entire political future may hinge."

Two weeks earlier, the federal-provincial conference in Quebec City had ended disastrously. Opposition Leader Diefenbaker reflected a growing popular opinion on April 3 when he said in the House of Commons that the conference had been a fiasco. The decisive sign of failure had been a separate press conference given by Quebec's Premier Lesage at the close of the conference.

"We must say that the government of Quebec is not satisfied," he had told journalists, "and that in the very near future we shall have to consider with unprecedented seriousness the tenor of the next budget speech."

No one in Quebec or Ottawa had difficulty translating this remark. Urgently requiring additional revenue, the Quebec government was about to impose some form of "double taxation" on its taxpayers and was preparing to transfer as much responsibility as possible for this unpopular action to the federal government. The result would be a breach between Quebec and Ottawa Liberals, serious damage to the federal Liberal party in Quebec, and a rift between English and French Canada that could only inflame extremists on both sides.

The situation merited the "crisis" description given by W. A. Wilson on April 16. But the correspondent of the *Montreal Star* could not know, because it was a fact then known only to cabinet ministers in Quebec and Ottawa and to a small number of civil servants in both capitals, that the crisis no longer existed on April 16. It had been all but eliminated the previous week.

The events of the week following the conference, although reported fragmentarily in the daily press, have remained a hidden but important chapter in the history of relations between Quebec and the federal government. They illustrate both the tenuous contacts between the men in power in each capital and the special quality of the relationship between the Pearson and Lesage governments which have given rise to the nebulous catch-phrase "co-operative federalism."

According to informants, the federal-provincial conference in effect ended a few minutes after it began on the morning of March 31, 1964, in Quebec's Legislative Assembly, well guarded, soundproofed, and wired for simultaneous translation for the first time in history.

Before the conference opened, it was known that Quebec had been working on its own pension scheme. Using the technique that had proved successful in the power nationalization program, the Lesage government had assigned an expert "task force" to the pension question in 1963. The group included Claude Morin, a former professor at Laval University who had travelled with Lesage as a speech-writer in the 1962 Quebec election campaign, joined the civil service in the spring of 1963, and in less than a year risen to the position of Deputy Minister of Federal-Provincial Affairs and a rôle of great influence both within the "Mafia" and at the Premier's right hand. Among the others were Claude Castonguay, a Quebec City actuary; Michel Belanger, a former federal civil servant who had become, as Assistant Deputy Minister in René Lévesque's Department of Natural Resources, another leading member of the "Mafia"; and Jacques Parizeau, a brilliant and apparently indefatigable economist from École des Hautes Études Commerciales, the commerce faculty of the University of Montreal.

The task force had compiled a formidable report on a pension plan designed to provide not only social security but an investment fund which the Quebec government could use to lessen its dependence on the usual private sources of money on Montreal's St James Street and in the United States. Some people in Ottawa had been given a general idea of this work in February, 1964, but there was a feeling among members of the task force that the informal leak of information had made little impression on the federal government, which was then involved in trying to formulate its own pension plan.

"We felt that Ottawa didn't take us too seriously," said one member of the group. "Seven weeks before the conference they knew roughly what our position would be. I saw [a member of the Pearson cabinet] ten days before the conference and explained as much as I could of what would be in the Lesage statement to the meeting.

"When the conference opened, it already was too late to do much on the pension plans. It wasn't the kind of subject that you could decide in a few hours."

The federal politicians had sufficient awareness of brewing trouble to attempt to delay discussion of pensions. When the delegates sat down on the morning of March 31 in Quebec City, Prime Minister Pearson suggested that they should go through other items first and postpone consideration of pensions until the following morning.

Everyone was agreeing to this proposal when a member of the federal cabinet turned jokingly to Premier Lesage and said, "Yes, but have you got anything to discuss?"

The pleasantry was lost on the Premier. Among the documents that he had brought into the conference chamber was the five-hundred-page report of the pension task force.

"Yes, we have something to discuss," he said, "and here it is."

The dossier hit the table with a thud. Lesage went on to outline briefly what was in it. It was then that Premier Smallwood asked archly whether it might be possible to get into the Quebec plan. There was another period of silence as Premier Robarts of Ontario started talking about "two standards."

When a certain province wanted to opt out of the federal plan, he said, it was accused of ruining the plan. But apparently it was all right if a certain other province wanted to do the same thing.

"Since we're making a few preliminary remarks..." said Premier Stanfield of Nova Scotia.

Said an informant later, "Stanfield talked about joint programs. Then Roblin of Manitoba brought up something about Quebec's system of paying allowances to university students. And the whole conference was finished. From then on, Pearson just sat."

The conference ended without producing agreement on pensions, Quebec's demand for a greater share of tax revenues, and other important items. The following day, in Ottawa, Prime Minister Pearson said that the federal government intended to go ahead with its own pension plan without delay. But at the conference Premier Robarts had announced that Ontario would enter the federal plan only if it applied to all provinces, including Quebec. There was widespread doubt that a national plan would be feasible without the co-operation of the two largest provinces.

This was the situation during the weekend of April 4 and 5.

"The gloomiest weekend I have ever spent," recalled a member of the federation delegation to the conference. "I began to realize that we had to do something or everything might go into a tailspin."

There were still a number of factors working in Ottawa's favour. The Quebec government honestly did not relish the prospect of lambasting the federal government in its forthcoming budget speech. It was a dangerous tactic in the volatile atmosphere of Quebec, a spark that might set off a chain reaction of unpredictable force. It also went against the grain of a genuinely cordial feeling that existed in Quebec toward Prime Minister Pearson.

"Pearson is the most wonderful man that I have ever met," said a senior Quebec civil servant. "At least he tries to understand. At·the end of the conference, when we knew that we would have to have a separate press conference and say things that would hurt Pearson, it was really sad for us to do it. We were ill at ease about it. We didn't care about the other federal ministers, but Pearson. . . ."

Said a Quebec cabinet minister, "Lesage realizes that if you can't get along with Pearson, you can't get along with anybody."

Beneath the wreckage of the conference, there was a faint hope in both Ottawa and Quebec, but particularly in Ottawa, that discussion of the pension and tax situation could be reopened. But by whom? This was the crucial question. Governments at loggerheads are like operatic prima donnas. It requires the ultimate in diplomacy to persuade them to even speak to each other again.

Despite the presence of seventeen French-Canadian ministers in the Pearson cabinet, relations between this group and the action group in the Lesage cabinet were weak.

Secretary of State Maurice Lamontagne, once extremely close to important provincial Liberals, had seemed in recent years to dwindle in stature both in Quebec and Ottawa. Justice Minister Guy Favreau, officially the senior Quebec member of the federal cabinet, was earning a reputation as the Pearson of French Canada for amiability, but he was regarded with some suspicion in Quebec because of his previous career as a federal civil servant. Immigration Minister René Tremblay had been Deputy Minister of Industry and Commerce in Quebec before entering federal politics but he was not remembered in Quebec City as the most ambitious or energetic member of the "Mafia." None of the other French-Canadian ministers were "in" with the power group in Quebec, with one exception. Maurice Sauvé, who had been named Minister of Forestry only on February 3, 1964, had retained a favourable image in Quebec since the fifties, when he had been public relations officer and a hard-driving worker for the Quebec Liberal Federation.

Sauvé had been instrumental in persuading Claude Morin, when he was still teaching at Laval University, to become involved in planning the Quebec Liberal program. He also was on good terms with Tom Kent who, as Prime Minister Pearson's policy secretary and one of the authors of the federal Liberals' pension plan, was playing a rôle in Ottawa at this stage which corresponded roughly to Morin's rôle in Quebec.

Between Kent and Morin, the former newspaper editor and former university professor, there were professional respect and a certain similarity of character. It was Kent, on the Monday following the break-up of the conference, who made the first approach to Quebec through Morin, an informal telephone call in which, during a discussion of other matters, he intimated that the federal government had not abandoned all hope of further discussion with Quebec on the pension plan and tax-sharing arrangements. In fact, Kent had been working over the weekend with Gordon Robertson, secretary of the federal cabinet, and had written on Monday a memo for the Prime Minister suggesting a new approach to the problem.

Sauvé, as a junior minister, had not been at the conference in Quebec City but had kept himself closely informed of its results. Now he began to see a useful rôle for himself. On Tuesday, April 7, the day after Kent's telephone call to Quebec, he phoned Morin for a friendly chat. This was the first straightforward discussion of the impasse between Quebec and Ottawa since the conference had ended the previous Thursday. Morin told Sauvé that he was working on the Quebec budget speech and that it was going to be tough on the federal government.

Sauvé knew that Pearson had scheduled a meeting of six or seven cabinet ministers at his home the following evening, Wednesday, to discuss the federal-provincial situation. But for the young minister time was of the essence. The situation was so critical that it was essential to reopen talks with Quebec as soon as possible. There was another reason for hurry which may or may not have occurred to Sauvé. Only if discussions were opened in a rushed emergency atmosphere would he be able to function effectively as a corner-cutter. The longer the delay, the more chance there was that negotiations would commence, if at all, at levels far above the office of the Minister of Forestry.

Sauvé managed to see the Prime Minister before supper on Tuesday. It was about 6.10 p.m.

"Well, Maurice, what's the new crisis?" grinned Pearson.

When he left the office at 6.40 p.m., he had obtained extraordinary permission for himself and Tom Kent to make an immediate and secret trip to Quebec City to see Morin. Originally Kent had intended to try to see Morin after the small cabinet session on Wednesday night, but he agreed to the earlier contact. He rushed home, threw pyjamas and shaving kit into an overnight bag, and dashed for the airport. But before he left, he telephoned Transport Minister Pickersgill, who was scheduled to meet Lesage in Quebec City the following day on another matter. It would have been impolitic to keep the visit secret from Pickersgill, who would be a valuable ally in the cabinet if a new deal were worked out with Quebec.

Sauvé telephoned Morin from the airport in Ottawa to inform him that he and Kent were on their way. During the flights to Montreal and Quebec City, the secret negotiators encountered what seemed to be hordes of acquaintances, including one of the sons of Premier Lesage. As soon as he landed in Quebec City the junior Lesage called Morin to warn him that Kent and Sauvé were in the city.

"Routine business," said Morin.

The three men met at 9.30 a.m. the following morning, Wednesday, in the Château Frontenac. They talked all morning and ate lunch in Kent's room. It was agreed that the two men from Ottawa would meet Premier Lesage in his office about three o'clock that afternoon. Lesage was accompanied by René Lévesque and Gérin-Lajoie during the meeting, which took place while Pickersgill was cooling his heels in another office. Unaware that Pickersgill knew of the meeting, Lesage took elaborate precautions to guide Kent and Sauvé out of his office by a devious route before he returned to the Legislative Assembly, waited for a few minutes, and then emerged to greet Pickersgill in an office near the assembly chamber.

Kent and Sauvé returned to Ottawa that evening in a DC-3 provided by the Quebec government, a good omen. They immediately went to the informal cabinet meeting in Pearson's home. For Kent, the hard part of the job was just beginning. He had to broach the matter tactfully to Quebec ministers who might be jealous of Sauvé's unusual role and also anticipate the no-more-concessions-to-Quebec grumbles which came, as expected, from some English-speaking members of the cabinet.

The rest of the week was spent in lining up support in the cabinet and preparing for a brass-tacks negotiating session with Quebec. Morin and Castonguay came to Ottawa on Saturday, April 11, and spent all day and part of the evening with Kent, Sauvé, and a team of senior federal civil servants. By the end of the meeting the two groups had worked out the general lines of an agreement which would enable Quebec to administer its own pension plan in its own territory and, more important, to have access to the investment fund built up by the contributions of Quebec citizens. The two men from Quebec flew home that night on a Department of Transport Viscount.

The agreement was discussed at a session of the federal cabinet late in the afternoon of Monday, April 13. Prime Minister Pearson telephoned Ontario's Premier Robarts the following day to tell him what was in the wind and on April 15 both Ottawa and Quebec cabinets were studying the agreement at the same time.

On the same day, Premier Robarts was telling an audience in Toronto that he was "prepared to sit down with the governments of Canada and Quebec to devise a contributory pension scheme that is truly national." The offer was superfluous. Letters went out from Ottawa to the provinces the following day containing the details of the agreement.

On Friday, April 17, newspapers carried reports that an agreement had been reached. The formal announcement was made by Prime Minister Pearson in the House of Commons on April 20. The agreement involved not only the pension plan but a major increase in the provinces' share of personal income taxes.

2. THE MORAL OF THE STORY

The most striking aspect of this story is the fact that Quebec was functioning, in fact and not merely in theory, as a nation within a nation. On pensions, it had been possible for the Quebec government to treat the province as an independent entity. A separate pension plan was not only within Quebec's constitutional rights and practical capabilities; it was even preferable for Quebec to have a separate plan with control over its own investment fund than to abandon the field totally to a centralized federal plan.

Because Quebec had drawn up its own plan in this context, paying only secondary attention to the federal plan, Ottawa had no alternative but to adapt itself. The actual negotiations stand as the perfect embodiment of the two-nation theory: the French-Canadian nation, represented by its own government, dealing on a basis of perfect equality with the English-Canadian nation, represented by the government in Ottawa. Even Ontario was informed of the negotiations only after they had passed the critical stage. As for the other provinces, they waited in left field until the issue was decided.

It would be risky to harp too strenuously on this point. There have been instances in the past of two-nation negotiations between Ottawa and Ontario. But as Quebec attempts to define its position in Confederation as a province, that is, in the words of Prime Minister Pearson on April 14, 1964, "in a very real sense . . . not a province like the others" and one whose "position is bound to introduce special features in federal-provincial relationships," there may be a tendency for the Quebec government to work out this special relationship in direct negotiation with Ottawa.

This will be difficult if the negotiations depend on politicians. It is almost a rule that when French Canadians move into the House of Commons, they automatically become almost estranged from the people in Quebec. They are no longer objects of primary attention. This has been particularly true in recent years. It has been said that French Canadians have two eyes, one for Quebec City and one for Ottawa, but that in the sixties both eyes are riveted on Quebec.

There are magnificent exceptions to the rule — the great French-Canadian prime ministers and the Quebec "lieutenants" that some English-speaking prime ministers have worked with. But the Pearson government has been unable, so far, to produce a lieutenant or even a corporal's guard to muster its forces in Quebec. Not that it lacked French-Canadian princelings with a taste for ermine, but the times were unpropitious for them. The Conservatives and New Democratic Party have been in the same boat. Réal Caouette, after he bolted the national Social Credit Party, was a living example of the strains involved in keeping a foot planted firmly on both banks of the Ottawa River.

"The real trouble is between the French-Canadian ministers in Ottawa and the Lesage ministers," claimed a prominent federal Liberal. "Despite party affiliations, relations between the two groups today are not good. Many of the French-Canadian ministers in Ottawa have a wrong evaluation of what is happening in Quebec. They tend to believe that they have a better idea of what is good for Quebec than the Quebec ministers.

"They resent people like René Lévesque because they feel that he has usurped the 'defender of French Canada' rôle that traditionally belongs to a French Canadian in the federal cabinet."

Said a member of the Quebec caucus in Ottawa: "Lamontagne used to have free entry in Quebec, but it is difficult to serve two masters, to be a federalist and provincialist at the same time. At the moment, Sauvé is the go-between. Favreau, officially the Number One French Canadian around here, is universally liked. He hasn't an enemy in Ottawa or Quebec. But his position now gets in the way. When it comes to meeting the important ministers in Quebec, Favreau visits, but Sauvé can still drop in."

At the same time, it appears that a new channel of communications has opened between the civil services of both governments.

This is due primarily to the rise of a new group and mentality within the Quebec civil service which corresponds more closely to the type of men and patterns of thinking in the Ottawa civil service. Some of the most influential civil servants in Quebec have come from the federal civil service, where they still maintain friendly contacts. But even in cases where there has been no previous contact, as between Kent and Morin, Quebec and Ottawa civil servants can deal constructively with each other because the Quebeckers now have an influence and self-confidence and technical skill which few civil servants possessed under Duplessis.

One afternoon when I was waiting to see Claude Morin in Quebec City, three magazines arrived by mail in his office. One was the Montreal separatist revue *Parti Pris*, the second was the Canadian edition of *Time*, and the third was the airmail edition of the *New Statesman*. This is the reading of a man whose horizons extend far beyond the Plains of Abraham and who can communicate on the same wavelength with a man such as Tom Kent, regardless of the fact that Kent's second language is German, not French.

Under the Lesage government there has been more and more opportunity for Quebec politicians and civil servants to meet their opposite numbers from Ottawa and from the capitals of the other provincial governments. It was Premier Lesage who initiated the idea of regular meetings of provincial premiers to discuss common problems. The first meeting was held in Quebec City in 1960 and the sixth in August, 1964, in Jasper, Alberta. René Lévesque has been extremely active in the Canadian Council of Resource Ministers, a unique group in which federal and provincial ministers working in the field of natural resources discuss common problems on a basis of equality, without any special precedence being given to the federal government. Lévesque was president of the council in 1963-64.

It was the Lesage government which created a special ministry of federal-provincial affairs in 1961, with the Premier himself holding the portfolio. This department recently estimated that Quebec is represented by ministers or civil servants on more than fifty federal-provincial committees dealing with various matters of mutual interest.

Quebec has maintained a clear interpretation of its constitutional rights, particularly in the fields of education and welfare, but it also has tried to avoid working itself into costly citadels of so-called autonomy, as Duplessis did on such matters as federal assistance to universities, highways, and hospital insurance. It has tried to find workable methods of co-operation with the federal government. This has been made easier by the new spirit of pragmatism in Quebec and the realization, on both sides, that what the Quebec government wants to do for Quebeckers is very similar to what Ottawa wants to do for Canadians. Often it is not a question of goals but of methods, and methods are flexible.

This is the way an important figure in federal Liberal circles described the new atmosphere of co-operative federalism.

"You can no longer treat Confederation as it existed in the nineteenth century, when you made a neat division of powers and governments stuck to their own spheres. At that time, government was relatively small. But today, what one government does affects the other governments and there is a great deal of overlapping.

"We tried centralization in the 1940's and 1950's and discovered that it was not politically viable. And in any event, it never really included Quebec. It was the federal government and eight or nine other provinces, and a Quebec that was separate from Canada in a real way.

"Now that Quebec has come into the twentieth century, another solution is possible. You have two levels of government which are both powerful and which respect each other but which are not separate. They have to work out a lot of things together. We already do much more consulting with the provinces than any previous government, and in this Quebec is an active participant.

"The trend has been toward decentralization and in following this trend, Quebec has become more like the rest of Canada. Of course there is a difference in the degree of assertion of provincial rights. Quebec is pushing harder than the other provinces. But the trend is in this direction anyway. And the social objectives in Quebec at the same time have become much closer to those in the rest of the country.

"The trouble is," he said, "that people are too fascinated by the machinery of government. This isn't the most important thing. The job of government is to find ways, sometimes peculiar ways, to serve people. You have to be pragmatic about it. The machine itself doesn't matter a damn as long as it works, as long as the net result for the consumer, for the ordinary citizen, whether he lives in Quebec or British Columbia, is fair and similar."

Education Minister Gérin-Lajoie, in a speech to the Canadian Club of Ottawa in June, 1964, talked about the need to "build step by step, dealing individually with each problem."

"This empirical attitude," he said, "seems to me not only easier than rebuilding everything from scratch, but also wiser and more efficient."

"For many years," commented a Quebec civil servant, "the attitude of Quebec was that the rest of Canada and particularly the federal government didn't understand Quebec and shouldn't mingle in Quebec affairs. When we came in, we agreed that they didn't understand Quebec but we decided that we should take a positive attitude and state what we want."

A French-Canadian newspaper editor added: "For French Canadians to make the best of Confederation, they have to be very refined and articulate. We can — to use an impolite term — blackmail Canada into a good many things, but we have to explain ourselves clearly and wait for the right opportunities."

In an important speech delivered at the University of Moncton on May 17, 1964, Premier Lesage explicitly described Quebec's positive and pragmatic approach to co-operative federalism.

Instead of offering passive, I might even say stubborn, resistance [to centralization], Quebec has now concrete solutions to suggest . . . .

Instead of a Quebec which one knew beforehand would be opposed to federal undertakings, today one sees a Quebec which goes beyond this quasi-traditional opposition, and which offers suggestions capable of solving not only its own problems but of facilitating the solution of those which the other provinces and even the federal government are facing. . . .

At no federal-provincial conference since 1960 has Quebec made proposals which it did not believe to be practical. We wanted our solutions to be realistic. And furthermore, we proposed them ourselves instead of waiting for them to come from the federal government or elsewhere, because we know that it is Quebec, itself, which must find the answers to its own problems.

It seemed to us that a criticism of the federal system would be sterile were it not accompanied by constructive suggestions.

It is safe to predict — as safe as it ever is — that this tendency in Quebec is permanent. It began long before the Lesage government took office in 1960, in a new spirit which began to appear in French-Canadian universities and particularly in Laval University, in the labour unions and certain newspapers and television programs, and in the small but influential magazines of the fifties. It increases with every growth in competence in the Quebec civil service, with every new tendency toward realism in Quebec's education system, with every graduate who emerges from Quebec's universities with a professional ability which will count far more in the development of his opinions than the injections of extreme nationalism which he might have received along with his education.

Its nemesis is not within Quebec. The real danger is that this new spirit in Quebec will be rebuffed by English-speaking Canadians who are still infected by fear of Quebec — a fear created in part by the former tendency of French Canadians to wrap Quebec in mystery and to treat it as a nation which no English-speaking person could possibly understand. This gospel has been rejected by all but the extremist groups in Quebec and it should be rejected by all sensible English-speaking Canadians. Quebec is not a mysterious threat to the rest of the country. Responsible French Canadians are speaking in the plainest terms today, expressing aspirations which are not only contemporary but shared by all Canadians. English Canada should not delude itself with fears of "surrender" to Quebec's demands. It should listen not to the extremists but to the men who actually are running the province and who represent a Quebec that is more pragmatic and reasonable — with all the Anglo-Saxon connotations that can be given to these words — than at any time since the Conquest.

10

✤

The Quebec Church

Among the many shifting centres of power in Quebec, the Roman Catholic Church is the toughest for a writer to deal with. To give a comprehensive picture of Holy Mother Church in La Belle Province in 1964 would require interviews with every bishop, superiors of most religious orders, hundreds of parish priests, and thousands of lay Catholics, not to mention the Holy Ghost. This is beyond the scope of this short book.

However, the Catholic Church was and remains the national church of French Canada. In any survey of the Quebec scene it must be mentioned, no matter how inadequately.

This is not the time to stumble through the maze of Church involvement in Quebec history. The Ontario Orangeman who wants to find examples of bigotry, short-sightedness, and unwise political involvement by the Church will have no trouble locating innumerable illustrations. He has only to ask one of the many French Canadians who specialize in citing chapter and verse to prove that the Church has been throughout history Quebec's worst enemy.

In his admirably dispassionate book on Quebec, Professor Raoul Blanchard touches on the victorious battle waged by the Church in the nineteenth century to stamp out the liberal and anti-clerical tendencies which were evident in French Canada after the French and American revolutions.

"At the end of the nineteenth century," he wrote, "anti-clericalism had disappeared, and liberal ideas with it. From then on it was established that the French Canadians would form a Catholic nation charged with a God-given mission, taking over the spiritual rôle that France had abandoned.

"This acceptance of a God-given mission ill-concealed the inferiority complex which from then on gripped the hearts of French Canadians."

But this *is* the time to clarify a few ideas about the Catholic Church in Quebec and particularly to correct the common assumption that the Church is an organism in which every cog moves in harmony with the dictates of a single big wheel.

The Roman Catholic Church, in its entirety and in a theological sense, is an authoritarian organization resting on the rock of papal infallibility. But this does not mean, as many assume, that it is single minded on every issue or that the Church within a given region of the world is a model in miniature of the whole Church.

The lines of authority in the Church extend directly from Rome to the bishops. In his own diocese, a bishop is answerable to no one but Rome, for all practical purposes. The bishop in the next diocese has no more authority over him than a bishop in New Guinea, regardless of whether he wears cardinalitial crimson.

Cardinal Léger's authority, for example, is derived from his office as Archbishop of Montreal. It is limited to his own archdiocese. If he wanted to reprimand the Bishop of Rimouski on some point, the Bishop of Rimouski could, and quite possibly would, tell him politely to mind his own diocese.

This is basic to any understanding of the Church in Quebec. From time to time, of course, the Quebec Church has been dominated by movements in favour of various policies and influenced by bishops whose energy and ability enabled them to sway their colleagues and the laity. It is certainly true today that a sermon by Cardinal Léger in Montreal or Archbishop Roy in Quebec City carries more weight throughout the province than the words of other bishops. But this does not contradict the fact that the Church basically is a patchwork of semi-independent dioceses whose bishops look directly to Rome and their own consciences for guidance.

A progressive young priest described how he has been permitted for years to speak in certain dioceses but excluded from others. In one diocese, he made his first public appearance only in 1964 after the ailing bishop had handed over control to a younger coadjutor.

Quite apart from its sense of divine inspiration the Roman Catholic Church is a group of fallible men and is subject to all the ills of any man-made organization: inefficiency, rigidity, individual pride and laziness, rivalry, and poor communications between the top executive levels and the lower strata. It has its reformers and reactionaries. Despite pioneering experiments in thought control, it has yet to discover a method of bringing all men simultaneously to one opinion on many matters, even within its own clergy.

Recent events in Rome, when dignitaries of the Church gathered amid microphones and coaxial cables to discuss policy and elect a pope, and when the inner politics of the Church became a common subject of journalistic interpretation, opened the eyes of many people to the diversity, debate, and evolution within the Church.

For those who cared to see, the Church in Quebec has exhibited the same traits for years. While the Church has been accused of living too comfortably in a corrupt political atmosphere, it was the Catholic University of Laval that became one of the most important centres of resistance to Duplessis and produced some of his most outspoken critics, including priests. An incidental but revealing development has been the promotion by the Church in Quebec of some of the most advanced ecclesiastical architecture and liturgical reform in Canada. From the Church in Quebec has come a cardinal identified in Rome as a leader of the progressive movement. From a young teaching brother in rural Quebec came the book *Les Insolences du Frère Untel* that was the most important single expression of discontent with Quebec's system of education and a primary factor in creating a climate of popular opinion favourable to reform. It is true that the anonymous "Frère Untel" was packed off to Europe after the book appeared, to further his own education, but it is also true that he returned in 1964 and was hired promptly by the Quebec Department of Education.

After the Conquest, it was inevitable that the Church in Quebec should become the "national church" of French Canada and that the line dividing the interests of church and nation often became blurred. The "universal" Roman Catholic Church in Quebec identified itself so strongly with a language group that English-speaking Catholics and English-speaking Protestants were treated almost as enemies within the state by some French-speaking Catholics.

The experience of the Church in Quebec has been roughly the same as in any country where its interests have been joined closely to those of the state. It gained short-term advantages at the risk of ultimate disaster. It enjoyed both the privileges and handicaps of an established institution. It became a vested interest, an obstacle to change, and a target for reformers.

It would not be accurate to say that in Quebec today one finds official but apathetic Catholics of the type so commonly encountered in such countries as France, Spain, and Italy. Catholicism in Quebec still has a quality of fervent personal devotion. But the average urban French Canadian, particularly in the younger generation, has a growing desire to separate the Church from the official life of his group.

Even ten years ago, after extensive research in the rural counties of central Quebec, sociologist Philippe Garigue, now Dean of the Faculty of Social Sciences at the University of Montreal, reported that "informants stated that a distinction was made by the people of these communities between religious and secular activities, and that interference by priests in non-religious matters usually was resented.

"However," he went on, "in many instances the informants were unable to make a clear-cut distinction between what they considered sacred and secular activities. Thus, in most communities, schools are staffed by members of religious orders, and all informants thought that education should not be entirely secular. The same could be said of political activities.

"While no parish priest had a position of political leadership, what individual parish priests had to say about licensing laws, the opening of a dance hall, or certain leisure activities, were often determining factors.

"It is advanced here that these are not traits specific to rural communities but are cultural characteristics valid for the whole of French Canada."

"In my own riding," said a Quebec cabinet minister, "I see the bishop about twice a year. We might discuss education in the local classical college. Maybe they plan to add a wing or something. We might discuss the local observance of the liquor laws. The bishop would ask me to see that the law is applied. I rarely see the priests in my own riding."

Educated urban French Canadians often mix anticlericalism with a sincere devotion to their faith.

"The average French Canadian took so much dirt from his clergy for so long that a reaction has set in," said a typical French-Canadian business executive in Montreal.

Another commented, "No wonder we revolted against our system of education. In the old days, we had —— all to do with it."

"Even in the unions, the power of the clergy is dwindling," said another French-Canadian businessman. "When the syndicat [French Canadian Catholic labour union] was formed at our plant in ——, the local priests were instrumental in getting it under way and were a radical element in it. Now a new workers' élite has taken over and the priests have lost power."

"The influence of the Church is going down but it still is very important," a French-Canadian newspaper editor said.

"A good example was the controversy over the original legislation setting up the province's first department of education. Certain bishops were opposed to it. I don't think that this alone would have frightened the government but it was worried about the possibility of the bill being defeated in the Legislative Council [Quebec's unique provincial senate] where a majority of members were appointees of the Union Nationale and opposed to the government.

"The government said to itself, 'If we pass the bill and run into trouble in the Legislative Council, then we might have to go to the polls appearing to be opposed by the Church, and we'll lose.' I don't think that the same consideration will occur to a Quebec government in 1970, but it is still there today."

Another French-Canadian journalist claimed that Premier Lesage, before publicly announcing his cabinet after the 1960 election, sent a list of proposed ministers to Cardinal Léger. According to the journalist, who claimed to have the story from Cardinal Léger himself, the Cardinal was embarrassed by the gesture and regarded it as unnecessary.

"Even today, quite a number of priests do not accept all the implications of what we are doing," said a senior civil servant in Quebec's new Department of Education.

"We feel subtle and strong resistance in many places. In the matter of regional schools replacing smaller local schools, for instance, the parish priests often will put the accent on the disadvantages — the need to travel long distances on school buses, the difficulty of supervising the conduct of large numbers of students, and so forth. The Church sometimes gives the impression of being more aware of the problems than the profits of the scheme.

"But I have a feeling that there is a distinction between generations in the Church. I have met quite a number of young priests, in the twenty-five-to-thirty age group, who resent the attitude of older priests on such matters as reform of the liturgy and changes in methods of teaching the catechism. When we speak of the clergy in Quebec, we have a tendency to lump together all sorts of people in clerical garments. In fact, the teaching brothers in our schools have always been more progressive than many of the priests in the seminaries. They are the proletariat of the Church, closer to the needs of the people than the priests living in the colleges.

"There is also a change in the rôle of the lay people within the Church. For a hundred years we have behaved as if the only way for religion to be transmitted was to keep it in the hands of the bishops. The recent Vatican Council, with its tendency to make the Church more 'democratic' and increase the rôle of the lay Catholic, is extremely important for Quebec."

"We are too inclined to say that the Church is not a democratic organization and use it as an argument to stop reforms," said a progressive member of Quebec's Roman Catholic clergy, who spoke with some admiration of the practice in some Protestant churches of issuing "calls" for new ministers selected by lay councils.

"There is no reason why some such system couldn't be introduced into the Church," he said. "Ideas such as this are met among some priests and laymen who see no reason why efficient means of democratic action should not be used inside the Church.

"One day, the decisions affecting a parish will be made not only by the parish priest but by a group which will include the curé, his assistants, and the lay council of the parish."

"People outside see the Church as monolithic," he continued, "but this isn't true. It doesn't correspond to the picture of the Church held by the French-Canadian layman. We live in a divided Church today, what you might call a two-level church, progressive and reactionary, and each level contains both priests and laymen.

"For instance, I feel that I am much closer to the theology of Gérard Pelletier [editor of Montreal's *La Presse*] and André Laurendeau [editor of *Le Devoir*] than to the theology of many bishops in the province. In the case of some of them, Msgr ——, for example, I feel that their concept of the Church is really wrong.

"Men such as Pelletier have managed to retain their idealism and remain within the Church. But for every person who has done what he has done, ten men have not done it and have left the Church in disgust. I think that it is stupid to see people leave the Church for reasons which the Church could eliminate.

"I don't think that there is going to be a break someday between the two groups in the Church but there are going to be strong tensions."

The Church in Quebec, despite changes, still awaits its version of the "quiet revolution." There are what a priest called "isolated pockets of reformers" within the Church, but they have not gained the control enjoyed by the reformers in the political life of the province. "Out with the old and in with the new" is a much longer process in the Church than in the political world. The only retirement which established dignitaries of the Church accept is the ultimate one.

"Within the Church," explained the same priest, "there are

different structures than in the outside world. It takes more time for changes to become evident. It is still not easy for a priest to express himself publicly. He has to be careful, partly to avoid compromising the Church and partly because the Church is still quite 'vertical.' In the diocese of Three Rivers, for instance, it is impossible for a priest to express an opinion at variance with the opinion of his bishop.

"In other dioceses, there is more of a team spirit. I have been in small dioceses outside Quebec where the bishop is more on a par with his priests. There's a simplicity that you don't find in Quebec, where bishops are often surrounded by many assistants who are just as reactionary as they are.

"Here it is exceptional to see a bishop meet his priests in an atmosphere where they are free to talk. He talks to his priests today but there is little discussion. I think that some of the bishops are afraid of what might happen if they started to loosen up."

"Pockets of reform." Within certain religious orders for instance, there have been important changes. A young nun spoke enthusiastically about the new "flexibility" within her order which gives its members more control of their own time. Hours of prayer, for instance, are less rigid and there is more opportunity for individuals to devote their time to intellectual progress in fields of their own choosing. Sisters are encouraged to attend outside universities.

"Frankly," she said, "I don't know whether I could stand living the way our sisters did fifteen years ago."

A young priest talked about a meeting in the winter of 1963-64 attended by chaplains of Catholic Action groups, including a number of university groups.

"For the first time in my experience," he said, "a great number of chaplains very frankly took positions opposed to some of the bishops. They were even willing to tell the bishops that they had no competence to discuss certain aspects of their work among the students."

Priests in Quebec read Catholic publications from other countries in which priests express views which would seem almost heretical in their own dioceses. A priest from France, so advanced that he got into trouble even at home, gave lectures at Laval University some years ago that influenced continuing work on the teaching of the catechism. Another priest referred to a friend of his, a young curate in Lauzon, Quebec, "who spends all his time with the workers, speaks like a worker, and has a progressive outlook."

"Something is happening, but from the bottom, not from the top," said a French-Canadian priest. "There are new relations springing up inside the Church. It hasn't extended far but we feel it."

There is also reaction. This same priest talked about an annual "open parliament" of Quebec priests interested in social action which had met regularly and freely until about 1956, "when the bishops decided to control the speakers."

"They then decided that it would be better to hold the convention every two years," he related, "and today the group is domesticated."

"The Church is losing influence, no doubt," agreed another young French-Canadian priest. "Before, there was too much mixing of what you might call the sacred and the profane. Now we are trying to separate them.

"I myself even think that non-denominational education by the state eventually will come to Quebec. You will continue to have private colleges, but in those supported by the state there will be only a few religious who are teachers and they will usually be teaching strictly religious subjects.

"But of course the government has a problem when it is trying to secularize institutions. What would happen if all the religious in our hospitals stopped working tomorrow? What would happen if they stopped teaching in schools, where they receive salaries which are lower than those of lay teachers? And often the religious teachers in the elementary schools are better qualified than the lay teachers. Many of them attend summer schools. It is easier for them to do this than for the lay teachers who have to work in the summer."

A survey of classical colleges in Quebec in 1963 indicated that it would increase their costs by about $10 million a year if they had to pay lay teachers' salaries to all their teachers who belong to religious orders.

"In general," the same priest continued, "the clergy is changing very fast, particularly those under fifty years of age, although it is dangerous to generalize about the younger generation. I was in a parish the other day where the curé, who was sixty, was very progressive while his assistant, who was thirty-two, was quite conservative. But on the whole, the young priests realize that they are not able to work in the temporal sphere as priests did before. They understand this, but, more important, they accept it.

"It also depends on the region. In some rural areas of Quebec that were settled only in the past hundred years, the Church automatically became a centre of influence. Sometimes bishops have taken over attitudes that suited those days without realizing that the situation has changed. And you find laymen who make the same mistake. In the parishes that are backward in terms of economic and social development, the problem is not only on the side of the clergy. When something has to be organized in these areas, the people automatically look to the priest. You can't do anything in the region without his co-operation."

"For those below twenty-five years of age, the influence of the Church is nearly zero," claimed a young Quebec civil servant originally from Montreal.

"Even in the practice of our religion, we are only mediocre. We are becoming more and more Protestant in our communications with God."

By "Protestant," he explained, he meant that religion was becoming more and more a matter for private decision. When the conversation touched on birth control, for instance, he said, "That's one place where the Church and I part company.

"The influence of the Church depends on the region. It is lowest in Montreal and highest in an area like the Gaspé. But you have to remember that the cities are being given a stronger voice in the legislature through electoral redistribution and that all the new important civil servants and the important ministers come from the cities. If they haven't been born there, they've been educated in city universities.

"When the politicians worry about the rural vote, I say, 'What rural vote?' The mood in small cities and large villages, thanks to travel and television, isn't all that different from the feeling in Montreal these days. Many of the so-called rural ridings today have large suburban populations.

"The Church still might influence or delay certain measures," he conceded, "it might make politicians do a bit of thinking, but it is not a very strong influence on government policies."

"The pressure of the Church is everywhere a thing of the past," said a cabinet minister, "and the Church accepts this. It is hard to explain this to people outside Quebec."

Added an English-speaking businessman in Montreal with good contacts in French Canada, "The Anglo-Saxon still doesn't realize that the French Canadian has completely abandoned his old dependence on the clergy."

The 1963 survey of classical-college students mentioned earlier in this book revealed that 601 of the 794 students who took part in the survey claimed that religion played an important rôle in their lives. This "positive" answer was given by 84 per cent of the girls and 72 per cent of the boys. In the "negative" group were eighty students who said that religion represented a problem for them, thirty-three who said that they were indifferent to religion, thirty-three who were anti-religion, and forty-seven who failed to answer the question: "What place does religion have in your life? Explain your answer."

This response, at first glance, might be less "positive" than a non-Quebecker would expect, but the 80 per cent "positive" response in an age group where rebellion is expected means that the Church still has a certain amount of time in which to adapt itself.

Emerging slowly is a "North American" concept of the Roman Catholic Church as a strong indirect force on events working through individual Catholics, both priests and laymen, rather than as an institution functioning almost as a minor government. This is another instance of the Quebec mentality adopting twentieth-century attitudes which are more easily understood outside Quebec. But the predominantly Catholic make-up of the Quebec population will ensure that the situation of the Church in Quebec will continue to be different than in provinces where the religious complexion of the population is more varied.

11

❖

"Capitalistes" and Anti-Separatists

Once upon a time there was a nice division of functions in
Quebec. The brain was English and the soul was French.
Business on a large scale was an Anglo-Saxon and Protestant
activity, while French Canadians were supposed to be reserved for some higher form of existence.

It is one of the ironies of history that those who preached
this doctrine, so convenient for English-speaking people, were
French-Canadian politicians and priests who seemed blind
to the increasingly obvious fact that the "higher life" of the
average French Canadian was spent in modern cities, where
he enjoyed all the disadvantages and few of the benefits of
industrial progress.

The classic formulation of the French-Canadian vocation
was delivered by the eminent theologian Msgr L.-A. Paquet
in a speech in Quebec City on St Jean Baptiste Day, 1902:
"Our mission is less to manipulate capital than to change
ideas; it consists less in lighting the fires of factories than to
maintain and to make shine afar the luminous fire of religion
and thought."

The trouble was that, even then, more and more French
Canadians were lighting the fires of factories, in a literal
sense, to keep the Anglostocracy warm and cosy.

It is not difficult to find quotations equally quaint but far
less antique. In 1936, speaking to a group called Jeune Commerce de Montréal, Canon Lionel Groulx, now an aging but
not inactive influence in Quebec, delivered himself of the
following clarion call:

... small industrialists, little workers, recapture the taste for patient work, for the object made with perfection and love. To mass production, oppose quality production 'à la française' ... convinced that the smallest French-Canadian employer works for himself and his own, that the small artisan working in the darkness of a basement does more for the emancipation of his nation than the greatest of our wage-earners in the service of a foreign company.

So much for the workers. Addressing himself to the literary spirits of French Canada, Canon Groulx urged them to "liberate the poems which await the hour of creation so that one day in the future this little country will be again free and beautiful and this people will feel, crying with emotion, the joy and grandeur of life."

Nationalists of this stamp, completely misinterpreting the inevitable trend of events in North America and their own province, sabotaged the efforts of their own people to react constructively to the circumstances of their life. Theirs was an attitude based on fear, the same fear of challenge and change that exists today among the separatists in both English and French camps.

Venerable as this enervating doctrine is, it cannot be traced back to the glorious days of the old French régime — a period beloved by Canon Groulx and other nationalists of his breed. The French discovery and settlement of North America, while charged with the partisan religious spirit of the times, was based on business, fishing at first and later the fur trade. It was only with difficulty that agriculture was promoted in the colony. The Laval University historian Msgr Arthur Maheux has written that "early settlers came here for commercial rather than agricultural purposes."

"The French were actually better suited traditionally to commerce and to the professions than to agriculture," he stated.

From time to time, particularly about the middle of the nineteenth century, warnings were sounded in French Canada which still have an astoundingly contemporary ring. In the February 5, 1870, issue of the magazine *L'Opinion Publique,* published in Montreal by Georges Desbarats, the editor, L. O. David, wrote that "to every race must be given the knowledge to enable it to exploit the riches and special resources which providence has given to it, so that it can accomplish its mission." He continued:

We must have a practical education if we are to be able to gain some of the advantages and the riches of our country and to play our rightful part in their development, in the great commercial and industrial enterprises. And we are condemned almost exclusively (in our schools) to Greek and Latin! We need mechanics, engineers, architects, educated businessmen. And we have nothing but lawyers, doctors and notaries! ...

What good is it for French Canadians to speak Greek and Latin if they are unable to fill lucrative positions, if they are refused the best jobs, if the doors of all the business firms, where our English compatriots find an honorable existence are closed to them? ...

We have said it before: if the government would only favor in a very special manner the industrial and commercial schools, if it would only make sacrifices, if necessary, in order to get competent professors, it would deserve the eternal recognition of the country. Our future is in the balance. If we continue to encourage a system [of education] which is so fatal to the best interests of our country and our influence, we will always be at the tail-end of the nations which occupy this continent.

This voice, inspired by the same adventurous spirit that enabled the French to adapt so well to the early life of exploration and trade in North America, was not the voice that was listened to in French Canada. The battle for the minds of French Canadians in the last half of the nineteenth century was won by those voices which had found tongue when the French fled before General Wolfe in 1759. They were the voices of retreat. They said, in effect: "Yes, we are running away, but notice how gracefully, how purely, how exquisitely we run."

Conrad Langlois, a young professor at Montreal's Sir George Williams University, described this inferior-superior attitude in an article in 1960:

After the Conquest, the French Canadians developed two psychological complexes: one of inferiority and one of superiority. Because they had been ruined and they had lost the control of their own economy, they came to believe that they were not good in business and industry. They became satisfied to interest themselves in agriculture, local retail trade, handicrafts, etc. At the same time, they became convinced that they were superior in spiritual matters and in intellectual and artistic activities. In short, French Canadians came to believe that they would remain inferior economically but that they were already superior in religion, fine arts, ways of life and human values.

Cut off from European resources, looked down upon from a great height by their own clergy, deprived of adequate technical and commercial education, the French-Canadian business class deteriorated steadily from the time of the Conquest until some point in the first half of this century. A scathing assessment of this situation appeared in the magazine *Liberté* in March, 1962, written by Professor Fernand Ouellet of Laval University's Faculty of Commerce:

Moreover, since 1784, the economic inferiority of French Canadians became even more obvious. French-Canadian businessmen had shown themselves incapable of adapting to new conditions prevailing in the fur business. At a time which demanded unified efforts and a concentration of capital, they remained resolute individualists. Their conservatism and their fear of risk dissuaded them from investing capital in new sectors of the economy. This orientation was such that at the beginning of the nineteenth century, French Canada lacked a class of dynamic businessmen capable of defining the objectives of their group in the light of new situations and not only in relation to the past.

The bitter battle against British imperialism helped in a certain measure to distract the attention of French Canadians from the vast problem posed for their society by the rapid progress of industrialization and urbanization.

*The development of hydro-electric and mineral resources,
the manufacture of pulp and paper, at a time favorable to the
influx of British and American capital, revealed still further
the economic weakness of the French segment of the population. Despite progress since 1840, French-Canadian society
had neither the technical corps nor the scientific or financial
resources which might have permitted it to play an important
role in the development of the natural resources of the province. . . .*

*Lack of daring, narrow individualism, the inclination to in-
vest in safe sectors, the difficulty of seeing far ahead, in addition to a spirit of routine and sumptuous tastes, were the traits
which one found among the majority of businessmen.*

If the French Canadians were able to produce few important capitalists, the Anglostocracy created, without meaning
to and without giving any thought to the implications of this
development, a growing French-Canadian middle class.

As long as French Canada was predominantly rustic and
religious, governed by a village élite of clergy, politicians, and
small merchants, the Anglostocracy could carve out their fortunes in the peace and quiet of Quebec cities dominated by
their own group. But in an industrial age, the carving of fortunes is not a one-man process. It requires vast quantities of
manpower, one of the few items of export that rural French
Canada used to produce efficiently.

From the beginning of World War I, large pools of manpower were concentrated in urban areas in the province, particularly in the Greater Montreal region. A certain number
of these industrial workers and some of the thousands of small
merchants, service workers, and minor bureaucrats which they
required, achieved a comfortable degree of affluence. More
and more of their children were educated to expect a higher
standard of living and social importance than their parents
had reached.

Thus the Anglostocracy fashioned the instrument which
could destroy not only itself but the Canadian nation. This
urban middle class has become the most explosive group in
Quebec. It has provided the bulk of support for the separ-

atist movement. Most of the leading separatists have been drawn from its ranks.

Careful French-Canadian observers have been aware of this development for years. Claude Ryan, now publisher of *Le Devoir*, wrote in April, 1950, in an article in the magazine *L'Action Nationale*:

Within this proletariat of the middle classes there exists, beyond all doubt, a sentiment of deep frustration shared by all its members and, among many, revolutionary aspirations.

The revolutionary threat posed by the working class has often been discussed. We should also speak of the revolutionary rôle which, in modern history, is taken by certain elements which normally would have formed part of the middle classes. Hitler was an unsuccessful art student. Mussolini was a former journalist. Stalin was a one-time seminary student.

Another French-Canadian editor said, "The doctrine of separatism is more advantageous for the bourgeois elements than anyone else. That is why separatism has little success among the mass of workers. I suspect that there is a kind of instinct among the workers which tells them that if they are to get a better deal for themselves, the country must create more riches. The bourgeoisie is interested in transferring riches, not creating them."

But the middle class in French Canada is not only generating separatists. From this group also have come the new technocrats of the Quebec civil service, the influential politicians in Quebec, and a growing class of executives and second-rank capitalists to match the already sizable number of French-Canadian lawyers, doctors, architects, and other professional men. The middle class contains not only the greatest destructive potential in French Canada but it is also the group which must provide constructive leaders.

Whether the young men emerging within this group today become revolutionaries or evolutionaries will depend upon their success in achieving individual ambitions. For nothing is more obvious, but more often overlooked, than the elementary fact that the French Canadian has a perfectly normal reaction to success.

English-speaking Canadians do not find it strange that material progress has considerably altered the complexion of Russian communism. They realize that a low standard of living is one of the basic sources of political radicalism in many Asian and African countries. They often profess to understand how the Negro in the United States sees equal and integrated education, freedom of social movement, and economic equality as inseparable goals. But for some inexplicable reason, English-speaking Canadians fail to draw the same obvious lessons from the situation in their own country.

Quebec is not located on Mars. It is a North American "nation." The French-speaking Quebecker wants the same things that an English-speaking Canadian desires — a good standard of living, suitable education, and as much political and economic authority within his own territory as he reasonably can achieve. If he does not get this, he reacts in a predictable way. He wants to change the system that is holding him back. If he does get it, his reaction is equally normal. He wants to hold on to it. He becomes a defender of the status quo, an opponent of rapid and hazardous change, what an English-speaking Canadian would call a "good citizen."

Unfortunately there are no statistics which will prove decisively that a growing number of French Canadians are earning more money and exerting more authority in business circles in Quebec. Practically every English-speaking Quebecker insists that they are. French Canadians, particularly French-Canadian nationalists, tend to deny it because it weakens their picture of English "oppression" in Quebec. In my own opinion, there has been a significant growth in French-Canadian financial power in the past twenty-five years.

In the first place, French Canadians now control through public ownership most of the major utilities with the exception of natural gas, services which at one time were the foundation stones of huge Anglocrat fortunes. The most obvious example is Hydro-Québec, created in 1944 by the nationalization of fifteen private electrical companies, and expanded in 1962 by the incorporation of another eleven companies. Its assets have increased from $144 million at the start to more than a billion and a half dollars in 1963. The Quebec government started to move in 1963 directly into the field of private enterprise, setting up its General Investment Corporation to invest public and private funds in private industry by expanding existing firms and creating new ones. Its most important project to date, announced in the fall of 1964, has been the provision and organization of investment for Quebec's first steel complex. When the pension plan moves into operation and starts to accumulate reserves, it will further shift the balance of financial influence in the Quebec government's favour.

Where ownership of private enterprise is concerned, the French Canadian is still relatively weak. It would be surprising if he had managed to strengthen his position since World War II at a time when an increasing percentage of Canadian industry was falling into foreign hands. In a survey of foreign ownership in November, 1962, the *Financial Post* of Toronto called the 1950's and 1960's the "age of the Big Takeover." It claimed that in 1960, foreign owners controlled almost 70 per cent of the assets of Canada's big manufacturing, petroleum and natural gas, and mining enterprises. According to the *Financial Post*'s statistics, 38 per cent of the capital employed in the pulp and paper industry, Quebec's biggest, was controlled by United States interests in 1959, not to mention British holdings. The ratio for mining, another major Quebec industry, was 53 per cent.

Although statistics such as these are a constant source of irritation in Canada, English-speaking Canadians at least have the consolation of owning what the Americans, British, and other foreign investors have left. By the time the English-speaking Canadians have helped themselves to these leftovers, there is not much food, except for thought, on the French-Canadian plate.

Humanly enough, French-Canadian capitalists have shown little more resistance than their English-speaking cousins to good offers by foreign investors. Even as this book was being written, J. Louis Lévesque, the current Rockefeller of French Canada, sold a controlling interest in a French-Canadian insurance company to American buyers. But at least Mr Lévesque probably will reinvest his capital in other ventures.

When the six Miron brothers sold their huge construction company in north-end Montreal to Belgian interests, the $40 million-odd they received for the company virtually disappeared from circulation. At the time of writing, it was commonly rumoured that most of the $20 million in cash which they had received was still sitting in the bank, almost four years after the deal was closed.

The hopeful aspect of the business picture in Quebec is the growth of public French-Canadian companies from expanding family-owned enterprises. One firm of young French-Canadian brokers on St James Street has put better than a company a year through this process for the past eight years. Its first was a finance company whose receivables have grown, in the past eight years, from $500,000 to approximately $13 million. Other companies included a wholesale and retail food distributor, steel products manufacturer, swimming-pool contractor, dairy, bakery, building contractor, and another French-Canadian finance company. Most of these firms had expanded from the retail level in Quebec, traditionally dominated by French Canadians with the exception of certain department stores and supermarket chains, into regional operations which outstripped both the ability and financial resources of the original owners. The brokers in Montreal helped to reorganize their operations and contact investors, many of them new sources of capital in the French-Canadian community.

"It brought me into contact with people I never suspected existed," said a partner in the St James Street firm. "In the last year, I've interviewed more than a hundred French-Canadian businessmen who wanted to discuss financial problems and the possibility of public financing. Sometimes they astounded me. A pipe manufacturer came in last year. He had received a one million dollar offer for a firm that he himself had built up. How was he to know what to do? After we had talked, he told me that it was the first time that he had ever discussed his business affairs with anyone but his wife.

"But there is a new type coming up. The owner of one of the wholesale grocery outfits we worked on, for example, attended some sort of 'supermarket university' in the United States. Before he put up a new warehouse in Chicoutimi he toured new warehouses all through the eastern United States.

"There's no doubt that private wealth in French Canada has developed tremendously in the past fifteen years. And it has produced a new generation of French-Canadian businessmen. We mix more with the other groups. We consider ourselves Canadian, period!"

He said that the Alouette Chapter of the international Young Presidents Organization (entrance requirement: to be president of a reasonably important company before one is forty years of age) has about twenty-five members, and approximately half of these are French Canadian.

"Old habits are hard to shake," he admitted. "There is still a self-consciousness in the average French Canadian faced with the prospect of doing business with English Canadians. Few of us, for instance, do business in Toronto; yet I found that I got a good reception in Toronto. In some ways, it was easier to do business with an Ontario institution than a French-Canadian institution. In Ontario, they have a more business-like approach — and of course, more money to invest."

"J. Louis Lévesque was so nervous that he used to bite his fingernails when he sat down at meetings with us," said a typical Anglocrat. "Now when he walks into a room, you can pick the b—— as a top leader. He's got confidence because he's a financial success.

"Once the French Canadians make it economically, the rest will fall into place. They'll forget about making us speak French. Hell, they know we *can't* speak French."

Said an Anglocrat manufacturer about his dealings with a large French-Canadian wholesale distributor who recently had bought up or squeezed out a number of small French-Canadian dealers in his field:

"It simplified our business. It's a darn sight easier to deal with that French Canadian, with his mentality, than a lot of little French-Canadian distributors."

He went on to say, "I feel that there's a lot of room for expansion in this province and guys like that are the ones who will make it. Who's doing all the travelling these days? Who's buying property in Miami? I'm telling you, some of these French Canadians are really on the move. But their own government is going to cook their goose unless it realizes that their own people today are doing darn well, and better all the time."

A French-Canadian economist predicted in 1960, "One or two Fords in the next generation and the economic history of French Canada might be entirely changed."

"There's a new kind of French-Canadian businessman these days," said a French-Canadian journalist. "The affluent French Canadians that I know are becoming more and more French Canadian. They aren't being assimilated. Twenty years ago, they would have sent their children to Loyola College or Marianopolis or even to one of the English-language universities. But today their children go to St Stanislas or Marie de France, then to a French-Canadian university, and possibly to Paris.

"If you train a man like this in his first twenty-one years, he's not ashamed of his culture. The French Canadians who went into business twenty years ago never possessed this. What they left behind had no value for them, so they became English.

"There really are two different generations of businessmen. At parties, you can pick out the two types immediately."

The French Canadian who feels secure against the English "contamination" of the business world is still a comparatively rare bird. Most of his compatriots continue to exhibit a traditional schizophrenic response in the face of contact with English-speaking people. They do not completely accept or reject them. Even families suffer from split personalities in French Canada.

"Cousin —— got pretty cosy with the English," recounted a member of a wealthy French-Canadian clan in Montreal, "but Uncle —— always stuck with the French Canadians. He used to say, 'Remember that your bread and butter comes from the French Canadians. The English will just use you. If you want to be a success, stay with your own.'"

This attitude in business was reflected in the 1930's in the "Achat Chez Nous" campaigns urging French-Canadian consumers to buy only from French-Canadian businesses. La Ligue d'Achat Chez Nous officially gave up the ghost about 1948, but its spirit produced a reincarnation of the old League in 1953 in the Conseil d'Expansion Economique. The Conseil hired a full-time director in 1958 and now claims to have 22 full-time employees and a budget of more than $200,000 a year from 1,200 paid-up members.

The Conseil is much more up-to-date than the old League. It employs modern socio-economic jargon when it talks about its three-phase program to investigate control of capital in Quebec manufacturing and retail trade. It has issued small pamphlets on banks and life insurance and general insurance companies which show, as one might expect, that French Canadians control only a small share of these businesses in their own province. In the summer of 1964 the Conseil was compiling a list of all French-Canadian-owned manufacturing firms in the province.

(In sorting out the ownership of firms in Quebec, the Conseil runs into problems which remind one of German attempts to divide Aryan from non-Aryan during World War II. During an interview, I asked the director of the Conseil to classify my brother's printing business. It was founded in France three hundred years ago and moved to Quebec shortly before the Conquest. From the time of the Conquest it has printed material in both languages. But most of its work today is in English and my brother's mother tongue is English. "There are a number of borderline cases," admitted the director.)

The Conseil's pamphlet on life insurance companies pointed out that Quebec citizens paid $1,290,000,000 in premiums to these companies between 1955 and 1959. Of this total, French-Canadian companies received only about $235 million. The other billion dollars paid to non-French-Canadian companies is viewed as "escaping" from French-Canadian control. This fact is matched with statistics purporting to show that non-French-Canadian life insurance companies employ relatively few French-Canadian directors, senior administrators, and actuaries.

The Conseil claims that its pamphlet on chartered banks resulted in the transfer of at least fifty million dollars in deposits from "English" to the two French-Canadian banks. The pamphlet stated that the secondary position of the French-Canadian banks "means the lessening of French-Canadian influence in the direction and control of national and international markets."

"One should be under no misunderstanding," it warned. "In our age, more than ever before, people are not listened to or respected unless they represent solid material strength."

In some ways, the Conseil's campaign resembles "Buy Canadian" and "Buy Ontario" efforts, except that it is based on discrimination according to racial origin rather than geography. The other side of the Conseil's "whitelist" of French-Canadian manufacturers is an invisible but implied blacklist of other firms.

Leaders of the Conseil have been at great pains to avoid being labelled as a blacklist organization based on racial discrimination. In a speech in January, 1964, the president of the Conseil, Sarto Marchand, president of Distilleries Melchers Ltée in Montreal, said that members of the organization "are not preaching racism or separatism but seeking the general interest of Canada." But the fact remains that the Conseil, despite its semantic gyrations, is a throwback to the old "closed" mentality of French Canadians. It is a rather unimportant backwater, isolated from the mainstream of Quebec's economic development.

Quite apart from the Conseil's work, the quickening of national spirit in French Canada in the sixties has had an automatic effect in favour of French-Canadian business. The Conseil's own statistics show that in 1960 French-Canadian general insurance companies increased their business in Quebec by 15 per cent compared with a comparable increase of only 0.1 per cent for other companies. But the realistic French Canadian knows perfectly well that, despite the increased economic rôle of the Quebec government and the growth of some French-Canadian businesses, Quebec will remain totally dependent on outside interests for a high standard of living and employment, as will the other provinces. It is in the nature of things that these interests are largely English-speaking.

Although Quebec was making great efforts in 1964 to interest French automobile manufacturers in locating in the province, there were no audible complaints when General

Motors announced that it would build a plant near Montreal.

Realistic French Canadians — which is to say, in 1964, the majority of French Canadians — realize that English will remain the primary language of business at executive levels of national and international concerns in Canada. They see no reason why French cannot be a normal language of business at the local level — why a French-Canadian factory hand should not be able to use his own language to his foreman — but they accept the dominant position of English at senior levels.

"This is a metropolis, not St Pierre Baptiste," said the French-Canadian manager of a large Montreal firm.

French-Canadian comments of this type are not difficult to find in the business world of Montreal. Take a young French Canadian, send him across Canada with the armed forces during World War II, give him a good job with a national corporation that requires a great deal of travel outside Quebec — and what have you got? Someone who speaks like this:

"Quebec leaders have lost sight of the fact that in the job that faces them, they need the co-operation of the rest of the country, through Ottawa. They haven't paid enough attention to telling the rest of the country that a sound Quebec is an asset to Canada." (In fact, when this interview was held in June, 1964, most of the important Quebec cabinet ministers were planning to do just that, in a series of speeches in other provinces in the last few months of the year.)

The young French-Canadian executive continued, "We should stress the economic benefits for the rest of Canada in keeping Quebec prosperous. After all, you can talk to the Anglo-Saxon on the basis of enlightened self-interest.

"Large corporations have a rôle to play. They can be extremely influential in bringing people to accept the French fact. Why shouldn't they put out all printed forms and literature in both languages, not just in Quebec but across the country? Sure it costs money, but maybe that's the price of being a corporation in Canada. Just getting people used to seeing French would be a big help. Right now, the people in other provinces regard anything French as unfamiliar, and you always fear what you don't know."

Companies that do this sort of thing do not always meet an overwhelming response. About three years ago, a leading Canadian bank sent a bilingual notice to its more than 25,000 shareholders announcing that its annual report would henceforth be printed in English and French. They were asked to mail back the card if they wished to receive the French version. Only two hundred cards were returned.

Listen to another French Canadian who occupies an important managerial position in a French-language Montreal company: "Duplessis had his faults but he was the chief and he ran the show. You need a central authority and the trouble is that today we have no authority in this province, anywhere. We have the rule of the minority because of the weakness of the majority."

When this man talked about the minority, he was referring to ultra-nationalist and socialist French-Canadian reformers. His majority included not only what he conceived to be the bulk of "sensible" French Canadians but also the financial élite in Quebec, regardless of language differences. He claimed that the minority, including most of the people working for French-language newspapers, radio and television stations, "has some kind of dedication to emphasize trouble." He criticized René Lévesque for irresponsible conduct. "If you're going to play baseball, you should be dressed like a baseball player," he said, "not a ballet dancer." But he was particularly critical of the Anglocrats for refusing to take a stand against the trouble-making minority.

"The English group was and still is the most powerful in the province," he said. "They have the power of money. They acquired it more than a hundred years ago because of hard work and the influence of the capital that they had. There was an eagerness in the Anglo-Saxon group to get ahead while we sat still for too long or our sons sold the businesses of their fathers to outsiders.

"Today the Anglo-Saxon takes a typically British attitude. 'Oh, it will pass,' they say. The English are very patient. They can hold out for a long time. But in this province, the English are a minority of such tremendous strength that they cannot let others settle the problem. They have to join with the moderate French Canadians and try to curb the revolution.

"Seventy per cent of the people in Quebec are just waiting to see what is going to happen. We businessmen have got to pay attention to politics or we'll be killed by politics."

This man had the North American businessman's traditional fear of socialism all wrapped up with his apprehensions about separatism. He was an exemplary defender of the status quo. His words could have been placed without much difficulty in the mouths of many Anglocrats, except that the Anglocrat would have accused the French-Canadian businessmen of failing to speak out and excused his own reticence by saying that criticism of separatist extremists by English-speaking Quebeckers would only gain sympathy for the separatists — an admission of his incomplete citizenship in his own province.

There were, however, in 1964, the first signs in French Canada of what might be called a counter-revolution. In my own opinion, the first wave of separatism began to recede in Quebec in the summer of 1963, when bombings by isolated and disorganized terrorists shocked French Canadians into wondering exactly where the roller-coaster of separatism was leading them.

A political science student at the University of Montreal told me that the climate there during the 1963-64 term had been much quieter than in the previous two years, although there was still plenty of excitement and the student newspaper continued to be dominated by separatists.

"We began to feel that we were going round in circles," he said. "The separatists had a solution, but after two years of debate we had examined the solution from every possible angle. We didn't seem to be getting anywhere. And a lot of us realized that separatism was taking up a lot of time and it wasn't the only thing in the world."

At a political policy meeting in Montreal in the summer of 1964, a party executive member about fifty years of age was talking about the need to give the program a nationalistic twist when he was interrupted by snorts of impatience from two unexpected sources, the president of the party's youth association and the president of the party organization at the University of Montreal. Said the president of the university group, "You'll never get any of my generation with that line. Can't you realize that what interests us is socialism, not separatism?"

The first concrete signs of change came in the spring of 1964. There was a highly significant fight in the editorial ranks of *Cité Libre*, the influential little magazine that had been an important liberal voice in Quebec during the Duplessis years. The original editorial group, led by such men as Pierre-Elliott Trudeau, now professor at the University of Montreal's Institute of Public Law, and Gérard Pelletier, now editor of the Montreal daily *La Presse*, had turned over the editing of the magazine to a younger group in September, 1963. In short order *Cité Libre* became so separatist in tone that the original group had to reassert its control six months later. It was galling for Trudeau and Pelletier, the angry young men of the fifties, to be cast so quickly into the rôle of outmoded conservatives by their young disciples. But Trudeau fought back by claiming that the separatists were the real counter-revolutionaries in Quebec who were betraying the liberal ideals that had motivated the originators of the quiet revolution.

In an article in May, 1964, in the purged *Cité Libre*, Trudeau bitterly ridiculed the "new dogmatism" of the separatists by claiming that they "wanted the whole tribe to return to the wigwams by declaring its independence." He said that they were "afraid of being left behind by the twentieth-century revolution" and lacked the courage to "carve themselves out a place in it by ability."

"That, of course, will not prevent the world outside from progressing by giant's strides," he reminded the separatists. "It will not change the rules and the facts of history, nor the real power relationship in North America."

In the same month, Trudeau and six other French-Canadian intellectuals published an anti-separatist "Canadian Manifesto." It was a remarkable document in that it was the first explicit and widely circulated attack on the separatists by a group of fairly prominent French-Canadian thinkers, two of them members of the faculty at the University of Montreal.

"Separatism in Quebec appears to us not only as a waste of time but as a step backwards," the manifesto stated.

"That [type of separatist nationalism would deliver but a purely judicial or formal sovereignty. The problem of real independence would remain untouched."

"Our view of nationalism is not at the present time shared by many of the middle class élite," admitted the authors of the manifesto. "But then again, nationalistic policies in Canada or in Quebec are generally advantageous to the middle class though they run counter to the interests of the majority of the population in general, of the economically weak in particular."

The importance of this manifesto was exaggerated in English Canada. After it appeared, the readers' columns of English-language newspapers in Montreal, Toronto, and other cities were filled for weeks with hurrahs from people who thought that it represented a reversal of policy among certain French Canadians. There even was talk about creating complementary manifesto groups in English Canada to join forces with the tiny band in Montreal.

Within Quebec, the manifesto created much less stir. French-Canadian intellectuals knew that it represented not a shift in opinion among their ranks but simply a crystallization of views long held by Trudeau and the other men who signed it.

"Trudeau leads a minority of one at the university," claimed one of his University of Montreal colleagues.

"His attitude is a direct result of his experience under Duplessis. In the old days, when there was conservative nationalism under Duplessis, those who were against Duplessis were usually anti-nationalist, with the exception of the people on *Le Devoir*. I think particularly of Father Lévesque at Laval and the people who worked with Trudeau on *Cité Libre*.

"Today these people do not understand what the new nationalism is about. Just because nationalism is traditionally reactionary doesn't mean that it has to be reactionary. The new nationalism is not reactionary, at least in most respects. It is part of our coming of age.

"It is hard for a French Canadian over forty to understand that the typical young French Canadian wants to free himself from foreign economic control, from capitalist control, and from Church control — all at the same time. People like Trudeau identify nationalism and separatism with a tendency toward revolutionary means and autocratic government. I think that he exaggerates."

Seen in its right place, however, the manifesto was an important document, mainly because Trudeau and the others felt that the spring of 1964 was an opportune time to publish it. They apparently believed that public opinion in the province was reaching some sort of turning point, or that it already had turned against the separatists.

A survey of 797 students in classical colleges in the Montreal area early in 1964 — average age, nineteen — showed that three out of four rejected the separatist solution as "undesirable and impractical." A typical response was: "It is better for the French Canadians to be fairly rich with the English than poor by themselves."

In June, 1964, in a special sermon in Montreal's Notre Dame Church on the occasion of the annual celebration in honour of Quebec's patron, St Jean Baptiste, Cardinal Léger delivered a rebuke to French-Canadian extremists.

"Between persons or human groups," he said, "the language of reason and of patience must be chosen in place of the recourse to force and violence . . . . John the Baptist told the soldiers not to molest anyone. The nation, then, of which he is the patron, must know how to show that it is not true that for it, force takes the place of right."

Warning that "no one can, in the final analysis, have any real and durable profit out of hate and social struggles," the Cardinal made a plea for pragmatism. He said that "a study of the exact nature of our cultural and political community is clearly a necessary preliminary . . . to determine and express, with the greatest clarity possible, the legitimate aspirations of the nation."

A few days later, on June 25, 1964, Marcel Faribault, president of Trust Général du Canada and a former secretary-general of the University of Montreal, delivered an even more significant speech before the annual banquet of the St Jean Baptiste Society, the largest French-Canadian national society, noted for following hesitantly but loudly in the wake of every nationalist movement that sweeps through Quebec. (If I were to compare the society with the Royal Canadian Legion in English Canada, it would be difficult to say which group would be more incensed.)

Mr Faribault told the armchair separatists in his audience that separatism was economically impossible and intellectually dangerous. He said that French Canadians had no alternative but to work as smoothly as possible with their neighbours in Confederation. "There is no other road to prosperity."

The extremists showed their appreciation of forthright comment by threatening to bomb Mr Faribault's home after the speech. Police kept an eye on the house that night and the telephoned threat was never carried out.

The *Cité Libre* fight was re-enacted on a larger scale during a strike and lock-out at *La Presse* newspaper in Montreal in the summer of 1964. One of the issues in the dispute, according to popular rumour, was the nationalistic tone adopted by some of the younger journalists. There were reports that the French-Canadian business community was putting pressure on *La Presse* to exert more editorial authority over its writers. The most obvious problem was a young reporter, Pierre Bourgault, who was elected president in the spring of 1964 of the leading separatist party, Le Rassemblement pour l'Indépendance Nationale. Bourgault was one of nine or ten known separatists, all under thirty-five years of age, on the newspaper's editorial staff of more than a hundred people.

Whether the dispute between journalists and management at *La Presse* is a valid example of anti-separatism is hard to say at the time of writing. The strike is continuing and the issues are complex. But a leading French-Canadian businessman said to me during the strike, "With *La Presse* gone for the past month, my friends feel that already it's quieter. You haven't got the same atmosphere to live in."

The danger inherent in the anti-separatist movement is that it will lead English-speaking Canadians, inside and outside of Quebec, to relapse into their former complacency.

They should realize, instead, that the stability of the province depends in part on the new class of politicians, civil servants, and businessmen who have risen, despite great obstacles, to positions of power in Quebec today. But these men represent only the vanguard. The growing middle class in French-speaking Quebec now is producing a flood of young men with great aspirations and, to an increasing extent, the education to warrant them. Whether these aspirations are satisfied or not will be the factor that will determine the attitude of Quebec in the last half of the twentieth century.

12

Unclear Power

In contrast to the long, violent summer of racial discontent
in the United States, the summer of 1964 in Canada was idyl-
lic. In Ottawa the politicians were in a lather about the new
Canadian flag, but the uproar ended at the doors of the House
of Commons. The only other place where one could encounter
interest in the flag was in the Royal Canadian Legion, particularly late in the evening after the bingo game. The rest of
the country was yawning. There was talk of a federal election but Canadians had seen so much of elections and election scares in the previous three years that they paid little
attention. The Royal Commission on Bilingualism and Biculturalism, after a preliminary round of public hearings across
the country, was preparing a new set of expense account forms
for the real round of public hearings across the country in
the winter of 1964-65. It was exceeding all expectations in ac-
complishing one of the main tasks of any royal commission:
boring the life out of a given subject.

The only explosions came from fireworks set off on St Helen's Island when the City of Montreal turned over the World's
Fair site to the public corporation that will operate the 1967
international exhibition. Expo '67 seemed destined to become
a healthy outlet for French-Canadian ambition and energy, a
useful employer of surplus manpower and a great soaker-up
of public attention. If it is a success, it will help to draw the
sting, as far as Quebec is concerned, from the 1967 centenary
of a nation which many French Canadians fail to regard as
an unmitigated success.

The calm summer period ended prematurely on August 29 when a small group of terrorists, trained at a summer camp in rural Quebec by a former French Army paratrooper, attempted to raid an arms store in downtown Montreal. One of the owners of the store and an employee were killed before police captured the terrorists.

The visit of Queen Elizabeth and Prince Philip to Canada in the first two weeks of October gave another publicity boost to the separatists at a time when their domestic audience, even in Quebec, was beginning to find them a bit tiresome. For weeks before the visit, British and American newspapers were filled with articles about the "Quebec problem." But the separatist demonstrations in Quebec City during the Queen's stay were small and disorganized — even ridiculous in the eyes of international correspondents who had covered civil rights demonstrations in the United States. It was reasonable to speculate that they had done the movement more harm than good.

In any event, most Quebeckers by then had come to accept this sort of thing as a normal if unpleasant manifestation of the real discontent in their province.

In the past, Quebec has been no stranger to violence sparked by racial animosity between English and French. One can argue with Hugh MacLennan's statement in 1959 that "in the last two centuries they have never seriously offered violence to one another." It all depends on the meaning of "seriously." Although there were political, social, and commercial as well as racial differences involved in the rebellion of 1837-38, and many of the rebel leaders were English-speaking, the fighting primarily was by English-speaking soldiers against French-Canadian rebels. It was serious enough to move a British officer to write that "all the fights have been in the churches, and they are now burnt to the ground and strewed with the wasted bodies of the insurgents. . . . War is bad enough but civil war is dreadful." Twelve of the "patriots" were hanged publicly. Discontent among the English-speaking population caused the riot in 1849 that, in the words of Stephen Leacock, left "the name of Montreal as black as the ruin of its Parliament." The burning of the Parliament Building and stoning of the Governor General disqualified Montreal forever as a national capital — fortunately. The conflict between English and French has always been too close to the boil in Montreal to enable the city to be a good seat of government, federal or provincial.

Despite this record, Montrealers of both groups were shocked in the spring of 1963 when bombs started to explode in mailboxes and against the exterior walls of federal buildings in the city. It was the first time that the racial conflict appeared to them in terms of physical danger. I myself remember how I felt on May 17, 1963, the day that Sergeant-Major Walter Leja was almost killed while trying to remove a bomb from a mailbox. It was one of the most depressing days of my life.

Montrealers who lived through that day never again will speak smoothly and confidently of the great amity between the two groups in the city. And the shock waves radiated from Montreal to every corner of Canada. Even a year later, when I was travelling for the *Montreal Star* in western Canada, talking with people in small prairie towns, the terrorism in Montreal came up again and again in conversation. It haunted Canadians.

No one, with the exception of a few nuts, condones violence. But it also is true that no one can ignore it. It was said in Montreal that every bomb blew another French Canadian into a vice-president's job. Certainly the bombs shocked English-speaking Canadians into at least thinking about the separatist conception of Quebec as another Algeria, as a nation writhing beneath the oppression of a foreign colonial power. This exaggerated picture contained a germ of truth: the idea that French-Canadian Quebeckers regard themselves as forming a definite national group. There is no doubt that the terrorists distorted the picture in Quebec and helped to create the "backlash" of anti-Quebec feeling that was evident in English Canada by the spring of 1964. But it is difficult to deny that their acts also had a constructive effect in shocking English Canada into a heightened awareness of the problem in Quebec and in hurrying certain attempts to do something about it. Possibly I can thank the terrorists for the fact that I am writing this book and that you are reading it.

In the summer of 1964, during the lull in terrorist activities, hopeful trends were continuing to develop.

English-speaking business firms were continuing to search for able French Canadians for their boards of directors and important executive positions. There was a feeling that, given time, the business aspirations of the French-Canadian middle class would be met by a combination of developments: help from the English-speaking business group, the growth of French-Canadian-owned business, and the growing economic rôle of the provincial government. The new mood of self-confident "pragmatism" among the élite group in French Canada could be viewed, although it was early to assess it, as the most important psychological change among French Canadians since the Conquest.

The Liberal governments in Ottawa and Quebec seemed able, behind a fog of theorizing about co-operative federalism, to evolve practical methods of co-operation in a number of important fields.

In the summer of 1964, there was growing hope that the development of the Quebec nation would not be on a collision course with Confederation but on parallel lines.

This hope was based mainly on changes within the élite groups in Quebec, within the power structure of politicians, civil servants, businessmen, and such opinion-makers as the press, television, and the Church. However it was much more difficult to discern trends within the great mass of urban workers, farmers, and townspeople in Quebec.

These people, with the co-operation of providence in depriving the Union Nationale of its only two effective leaders, had elected the Lesage Liberals in 1960 and given political expression to the quiet revolution. It was this same group which kept the province stable in 1963 when the French-Canadian élite, particularly the intellectual élite, was being mesmerized by the voices of its own separatists. Up to now, the separatist movement has been limited virtually to the upper and upper middle-class levels of the French-Canadian social iceberg in Montreal. Apart from the response of a very few terrorists and fascists and hooligans in the Montreal working-class, the average urban French Canadian has remained indifferent to the separatists' appeals. The response in rural areas, where Montreal intellectuals traditionally are viewed with deep suspicion, has been even more discouraging for the separatists. This is why the separatist parties, frustrated in their ambition to form a strong popular front, have been consumed by discord within their ranks.

But it was also this same group which gave Réal Caouette and his Créditistes twenty-six federal seats in the election of June 18, 1962. Historians may judge this event to be more important in the sixties than the separatist wave, for the separatists were only developing, in the context of the worldwide enthusiasm for national independence which followed World War II, a policy which certain people in French Canada had always viewed as an alternative to Confederation. There was nothing new about the idea of separatism. But Caouette was new and significant because his success was a pure expression of French-Canadian discontent. It was totally negative and destructive. He was not against Ottawa but against anything — federal monetary policies, high interest rates, nuclear weapons — which he interpreted as contributing to French-Canadian poverty. He promised "not bombs but bread and butter," although how he was going to do this was never too clear in the minds of his howling supporters.

The party fell apart, or appears to have fallen apart at the time of writing, because it lacked a coherent policy and strong leadership and because it was opposed in the election of 1963 by the combined strength of federal and provincial Liberals in Quebec. Even then, while losing seats, it increased its popular vote. But in its heyday it was a genuine popular movement, well-supported by the French-Canadian public and expressing their general dissatisfaction with the way things were going.

Anyone who heard Caouette exhorting a French-Canadian crowd in rural Quebec, playing masterfully on its discontent, drawing howls of anger or ridicule from it at will, had no doubt that he was seeing the confused manifestation of a power which could wreck the province were it to reach sufficient strength or be harnessed by a demagogue of more intellectual ability and staying power than Caouette. In the past two years, recollections of Caouette's appeal made one wonder what would happen if this spirit ever were tapped by a popular separatist leader.

This was the subject touched upon, indirectly, by a young *La Presse* journalist, Jacques Guay, in an article in *Le Magazine Maclean* in February, 1964. It was one of the quiet revolution's angriest pieces of journalism, but it was aimed, surprisingly, at the separatists. A few selections give the general tone and idea:

I am fed up. Fed up with the quiet revolution. Fed up with the leftists and their verbal anger. Fed up with René Lévesque and his hangers-on. . . . In short, fed up with all those who resolve the problems of Quebec from a great height. . . . The greatest obstacle to the revolution is paper. . . . The Left in Quebec is composed, with some exceptions, of a handful of impotent people suffering from chronic intellectualism. . . . Present in all the drawing rooms, bars and popular cafés, they infest the cocktail circuit, the openings of art exhibitions and the literary launchings. . . . On occasion, they transport their placards from Montreal to Quebec City. . . . But don't expect to find our Left at Saint-Tite-des-Caps, at Saint-Joachim-de-Tourelle, at Saint-Gédéon-de-Beauce, or in any other place located in an underdeveloped region. The "damned" ones of the earth and the sea know only two parties which speak their language, the Union Nationale and Crédit Social. . . . The quiet revolution satisfies only the bourgeoisie. . . . Those who have nothing to lose, gain nothing. . . . The only contact that the Liberal party maintains with the people is through the odious channel of patronage. . . . The great advantage [of Social Credit] was that it understood what our "great revolutionaries" refuse to admit, that to know what the people want, it is necessary to go to the people.

Guay is somewhat unjust. The Liberal Party in Quebec, by making scientific surveys of public opinion before elections and by trying to operate a democratic organization, has attempted to go to the people to an unprecedented extent. The young men of the BAEQ in the Gaspé, mentioned by Guay in his article, are going to the people in a calculated effort to assess their problems and needs unemotionally and to propose workable solutions. But where Guay is right on target is in sensing the gap which still separates the élite from the masses in Quebec, the lack of democratic animation in the lower levels, the dangerous distance between the "haves" and the "have-nots" within the French-Canadian group in Quebec, the dissatisfaction and frustration among the "have-nots," and the uneasiness which these factors create in anyone who thinks about the future of Quebec, or Canada.

13

Nationalism

Quebec is not, like the other provinces, a part of a greater Canada, at least not in the eyes of its French-speaking citizens. It is a nation unto itself, a nation which never has acquired the exterior trappings of nationhood but which assumes the more important interior qualities of a nation in the minds of its people. Despite alien penetration, it is united by a common language and culture, a common religious heritage, and a sense of common destiny.

Other provinces are part of a larger nation.

For example, if Manitoba today were confronted with a choice, if it could be proved beyond doubt that the national good demanded some sacrifice of important Manitoba interests, Manitoba would accept the sacrifice. So would Newfoundland or the Maritime Provinces, partly for financial reasons but mainly because there is a common belief that independence is impractical and that federation with some continental power is essential. Even British Columbia, where people live American and think British — or think that they do — subscribes to the primacy of national interest.

It is true that regionalism is highly developed in Canada. Secessionists in the Maritime Provinces always have regarded Confederation as a low-down plot. British Columbia is separated from the rest of the country by mountainous differences. Even on the prairies, where a racial mosaic has produced the closest thing to pan-Canadianism, there is a traditional suspicion of central Canada summed up in the cuss phrase: Bay Street. But separatism in Quebec, not official political separatism but the constant sense of belonging to a separate group, is far removed from regionalism. It is an authentic nationalism, warring continually in the heart of almost every French Canadian with his sense of loyalty to the Canadian nation. This makes it frightening to contemplate what might happen if ever an essential Quebec interest were threatened by Confederation.

It is necessary to say that *almost* every French Canadian places Quebec before Confederation. There are a few exceptions to the rule. From time to time one encounters a "Canadian" French Canadian, not the fraudulent exported article that is politely Canadian at cocktail parties in Toronto and fiercely Quebec nationalist in Montreal, but the real thing. Usually he is a successful French-Canadian businessman and his patriotism is rooted in this success. He does not like the idea of change.

However, the facts of commercial life in Quebec have dictated that this type of French Canadian is rare. The capitalist class in French Canada is not only underdeveloped but hampered by the fact that the largest capitalist group is English speaking. French-Canadian businessmen who try to exert a moderate influence on the course of events in Quebec are branded as "vendus." They have sold out to the English. Fear of being labelled in this way is enough to make most of them shut up. If they dare to speak out, the label prevents many French Canadians from giving their remarks serious thought. One of the major tragedies of the split social structure in Quebec is that people who attempt to take an independent line, differing from their own group's commonly accepted policy, are suspected immediately of being traitors. There is no neutral ground or, more accurately, neutral ground is that place between the lines where the fire of both sides converges.

Non-Quebeckers tend naturally to see Quebec in their own terms. They know that there are separatists in the province. They assume that other French Canadians either are neutral or anti-separatist.

This neat classification misses the basic point completely. Quebec is not composed of a "Quebec First" element opposed by a "Canada First" element. With the exception of the English-speaking minority, Quebec is populated almost entirely by the "Quebec First" element.

Opposition to official separatism in Quebec rarely stems from any regard for the Canadian nation. It comes from those who are as deeply committed to the "Quebec First" philosophy as the separatists but who believe that separation from the rest of Canada would be against the interests of Quebec. Always the future of Quebec takes precedence over the future of Canada. The nation to which every French Canadian feels that he belongs — feels strongly in a way that English-speaking Canadians can only envy — is the supreme community.

French Canadians who earnestly are attempting to formulate their approach to Confederation today are exasperated by English-Canadian attempts to classify them neatly as separatists or anti-separatists. The French Canadian himself is conscious of no such clear-cut division. He recognizes, in the official separatist, a brother "Quebec Firster" whose goal is the same as his: the development of the French-Canadian group. If non-Quebeckers could accept the fact of this universal desire among French Canadians, if they could stop trying to slap the separatist label on Quebeckers, if they could forget about trying to make emotional distinctions between the good guys and the bad guys in Quebec, the dialogue with French Canada might proceed on a more realistic basis.

English-speaking Canadians approach the provinces through Confederation. French Canadians approach Confederation through Quebec. In the section on "Government and Administration" in the 1963 edition of the *Quebec Yearbook*, the first paragraph contains a clear statement of this philosophy:

Quebec is a State with limited jurisdiction which, designated as a province, participates in the Canadian Federation.

First: Quebec, the national state of French Canadians. Second: Quebec participating in Confederation. What other province would see itself in this way, as a basically distinct unit which deigns freely to participate in Confederation? For the

other provinces, Confederation is dogma. For Quebec, it is a
proposition.

"Le Québec fait partie de la Fédération canadienne à titre
de province." Quebec *participates* in the Canadian federation.
It is in the present tense, not the past. It is a continuing act
of faith.

The import of this statement is clear, and it is no idle theory
dreamed up in the political science department of a Quebec
university. It is an official statement of government policy
drawn up by, among others, Claude Morin, one of Premier
Lesage's closest advisors.

The paragraph continues:

*Quebec is also the national state of French Canadians. In
fact, it exercises its government, within the limits of its jurisdiction, on the majority of the descendants of the original co-
lonizers of New France and over the territory in which they
are settled.*

Mercier, Taschereau, Duplessis, and now Jean Lesage have
all been governed by this philosophy in their approach to the
federal government. Non-Quebeckers often see the battle for
"autonomy" only in financial and political terms, as if Quebec leaders could possibly use the same gimmick year after
year if it were not grounded in some consensus of opinion in
French Canada. Men such as Duplessis might have misused
the national spirit of Quebec to bolster their own political
power, but they did not invent it.

"The vocabulary changes, the style varies according to the
time, but the fundamental principle remains the same," said
Premier Lesage in his 1962 budget speech.

"In a phrase, men pass away but the battle for autonomy
continues. It stands as a constant in the history of Quebec —
the 'autonomist constant.' And even though the governments
of other provinces consented in practice to become the 'pre-
fectures' of the federal government, the government of Quebec defended its autonomy just as energetically, maintaining
thus the right of existence of a nation of which it is the political expression and of which it remains the principal instrument
of economic self-assertion and cultural development."

To accept the reality of this "Quebec First" spirit within French Canada is not a concession. There has been far too much talk in English Canada about "knuckling under" to Quebec — talk based purely on an emotional reaction which might be considered strange in a people who pride themselves on Anglo-Saxon pragmatism. In fact, English-speaking Canadians would do well to examine their traditional image of themselves as the cool-headed, practical party in the dispute with the "fiery" French Canadians. There is emotion on both sides. The English-speaking Canadian naturally reacts to the notion of French-Canadian nationhood because it conflicts with, and seems to threaten, his own sense of national identity.

But surely their own feelings about Canada should lead English-speaking Canadians to appreciate the French Canadian's commitment to Quebec. Compared with Quebec, Canada is a young nation. Its people have no common background, religion, or long-standing national tradition. They have been drawn from almost all the nations of the world and the process of assimilation, in many cases, has just begun. Despite this, Canadians outside Quebec feel strongly and worry continually about their existence as a distinct national group. How much more understandable is the Quebecker's sense of membership in a national group united by tradition, language, and common religious background. This is a much tighter and more unified national group than the larger Canadian group.

French Canada's sense of national identity is rooted in history. Even before the Conquest in 1760, Frenchmen living in the New World had developed certain characteristics which set them apart from their European brothers. In Quebec, European Frenchmen began to encounter the same sort of hostility that later greeted supercilious Britishers seeking easy fortunes in Ontario or the Prairie Provinces.

In 1754, on the eve of the Conquest, Bougainville, an aide-de-camp to General Montcalm, reported of the people of New France that "it seems that this might be another nation and even an enemy."

The Conquest suddenly placed the survival of this group in doubt.

At first the British toyed with a policy of eventual assimilation. Then, for a variety of political, practical, and idealistic motives, they gave the French Canadians sufficient rights of language and religion and political representation to arm them to fight for survival. But it is too much to expect that the British in the eighteenth century would have tried to guarantee this survival, to introduce what we today would call a nation-wide policy of bilingualism and biculturalism.

The British policy was a typical compromise and, in the light of events, a failure. The present unsatisfactory state of affairs in Canada stems from the attempts of the British to have the best of both worlds, French and English. In some respects the British did get the best of both worlds, particularly in two world wars, but their legacy to Canada was two nations which have never been able to give their best to each other.

There is no need here to wade again through the post-Conquest history of French Canada. The dying Wolfe inflicted an almost mortal wound on French Canada in 1759 when he sent his redcoats over the top on the Plains of Abraham. It has taken two centuries for French Canada to recover, convalesce, and attempt to live confidently again.

French Canada, turning its back on the North American world, curled around its defeat like a pierced caterpillar. Beyond its ken a continent began to hum with the sound of machinery, in factories and fields, and slowly the babble of immigrant tongues blended into regional dialects of English. Within the charmed circle of French Canada, there were language, religion, civilization (for a few), poverty (for many), political corruption, and bitterness. Long after the Wolfe-inflicted wound healed, the caterpillar remained curled up. After two centuries, uncurling had become almost unthinkable.

If you do not care for caterpillars or analogies, Louis Hémon used the full literary orchestra about fifty years ago to say the same thing in his novel *Maria Chapdelaine*:

> Strangers arrived all around us, people that we liked to call uncivilized. They took almost all the power. They acquired almost all the money. But in Quebec, nothing changed. Nothing will change because we have a message to bear before the world.

*About ourselves and our destiny, we understood clearly on-
ly this task: to persist, to continue. And we have endured, so
that possibly in several centuries the world will yet turn toward us and say: This is the race which did not know how to
die. . . .*

The history of French Canada, like the history of any nation, cannot be symbolized by a straight line. There were
many deviations from the "closed" approach to national survival. In the years preceding Confederation, the caterpillar
from time to time uncurled cautiously. There were French-
Canadian politicians who urged their countrymen to take a
firm grip on the rights guaranteed by the British, men such
as Louis-Joseph Papineau who, as Speaker of the House of
Lower Canada in 1820, called on his people to "act like British subjects and free men." Some of the political leaders who
represented French Canada in the Confederation negotiations,
and in the years following 1867, believed that the new formu-
la provided for meaningful co-operation between English and
French.

But circumstances worked against a rebirth of French Canada to coincide with the birth of Canada. Other English-speaking provinces joined Confederation. The dream of French-
Canadian domination, or at least equality, on the western
prairies disappeared when Louis Riel blended survival of the
half-breed Métis nation, the French language, and Roman
Catholicism into a potent concoction that poisoned the Métis
and destroyed his own precarious existence as a rational
creature.

French Canada did not drop its guard at the time of Confederation and subsequent events convinced it that the dice,
all along, had been loaded against it. Polite talk about the
partnership of the two founding groups meant little when
bilingualism was an everyday fact only in Quebec and only,
to a great extent, among French Canadians; when it required
years of agitation to achieve such a trifling "concession" as
French terminology on federal government cheques, so many
years that the final decision was greeted in Quebec with more
cynicism than jubilation; when English-language Protestant

schools were supported by taxes in Quebec while Catholic schools in most other provinces were cut off from tax support and English was legislated as the only official language of instruction; when bilingualism in the federal civil service applied only to French Canadians; when, in brief, English Canada let nature take its course in an English-speaking continent without making many special efforts to provide for its special situation.

French Canadians are not the only ones who have emerged from almost a hundred years of Confederation with a host of complexes. English-speaking Canadians also carry psychological scars which make it difficult for them to approach the current situation impartially and in a spirit of perfect justice.

If the French Canadian's experience of Confederation is a bitter one, the other side of the coin might well be a feeling of guilt on the part of English-speaking Canadians. English-speaking Canadians believe that they have respected the letter of the law in Confederation. But many of them also suspect that they have used their majority position in nine provinces to assert the domination of their own group; that they have acted if not illegally, at least highhandedly on occasion in imposing their views on a minority group.

There is also in English Canada a certain feeling of resentment against the fact of being stuck with Quebec. Everything would be so much simpler if there were only one language, if only every Canadian were committed to building a single, homogenized Canada.

Strong feelings on both sides complicate encounters between English and French in Canada. This is why French Canadians constantly complain about feeling ill at ease in English Canada, in their own country.

"Why is it that I don't feel at home in other provinces?" asked a typical Montreal French-Canadian businessman.

"In Toronto, Winnipeg, or Vancouver, if I speak French, even if I speak English, I have a feeling that I am out of place as soon as I open my mouth. I don't have this feeling in New York. Even in London, I am more at home than in Toronto."

The New Yorker or Londoner can respond easily and naturally to a French Canadian because he couldn't care less about the French-Canadian "problem." But the English-speaking Canadian has been involved for generations with the French Canadian. He reacts to him in a special way and this reaction reveals, in a negative sense, the existence of a nebulous Canadian nationalism which encompasses both groups. Their mutual sense of irritation with each other, the fact that they often are uncomfortable in the presence of the other group, springs from some deep sense of common involvement.

If English-speaking Canadians have never fully appreciated the basic "Quebec First" sentiment in Quebec, French Canadians on their part have made little effort to discover the depth of national feeling in some parts of English Canada. They tend to equate regionalism in English Canada with nationalism in Quebec and to believe that English Canadians have little common loyalty to the federal nation. They overestimate the British complexion of English-Canadian nationalism, and the American complexion of English-Canadian life, failing to realize that the thread which binds British Columbia to Newfoundland cannot be regarded as non-existent merely because French Canadians find it difficult to see.

However the most important factor at the moment is not the Quebecker's picture of Canada or the English-speaking Canadian's picture of Quebec, but the Quebecker's assessment of his own situation. At the moment, he is utterly concerned with his own group. He wants to do what is best for Quebec.

Seen in this light, as a human being primarily and naturally concerned with his own welfare and the welfare of his group, the French Canadian is not difficult to understand. He is human. His reactions are normal. He functions in a reasonably predictable way.

That the French-Canadian Quebecker is a human being is one of those great obvious truths, like God, which most people accept but few act on. For two centuries, the French-English debate in Canada has taken place in a cloud of mystery. Each group is supposed to possess characteristics beyond the comprehension of the other. Even English-speaking Quebeckers who have lived their entire lives in Quebec will say such things as, "Of course, I don't really understand the French Canadians," as if they were talking about some tribe in the interior of New Guinea. The discussion is carried on in terms of "they" — and "les autres" always possess characteristics not only strange but fearsome.

The fact is, to inject another platitude into the discussion, that French Canadians and English-speaking Canadians are more alike than different. Their attitudes are rooted in the same Western European Christian tradition and shaped by a common North American existence which differs little, in externals, from one part of the country to another. They are of the same colour. Compared with people separated by striking physical differences, they can move relatively easily between the two groups. The number of French-speaking Mackenzies and English-speaking Gagnons in Quebec testifies to this.

There is no mystery about French Canada. As individuals and as members of a group, French Canadians function in ways that are quite comprehensible to English Canadians if the circumstances of their history and everyday life are understood. The only excuse for labouring this obvious point is that it obviously is not apparent to most Canadians. We still try to psychoanalyse each other as if there were some elusive key which one day will open the door of understanding between the two groups.

The only key is a sincere effort to see each other as reasonable people driven by the same motives toward the same goals.

POSTSCRIPT

When a writer is working on a subject, he becomes so involved in it that nothing else matters. During the four months which I devoted to this short book, the problem of separatism overshadowed everything else. This was not necessarily bad. My own preoccupation reflected the mood of my province for the previous three years.

However, it is probable that in another few years the perspective in Quebec will shift again. We might even laugh a little at the enthusiasms and the terrors of the early sixties.

As I was finishing this book, I received a letter from a Montrealer of my own age which effectively broke my own mood of preoccupation.

David Martin has been totally deaf since childhood. This enables him to look in a somewhat detached way on events which overpower most of us with their noise and confusion. The letter struck me so forcibly that I want to close this book by quoting a few paragraphs:

I have a theory about Canadians.

This country has had too little trouble within itself in the course of becoming a nation, and so when any piddling little thing comes up, like the conscription crisis or the FLQ or whatnot, we tend to make a lot of it.

We have not had enough firing and tempering in the forge where nations are made for us to realize how fortunate we are and how little we really have to complain about. Had we been pounded and hammered with a real civil war that involved the whole country and not merely a neighborhood, then we would have had the essential catharsis that would have left our problems as a people resolved. But having had too little trouble, our relatively minor naggings have remained, like a long-ingrown toenail.

The FLQ terrorist bombings are something that almost every other country in the world would sneer at. They would ask us why we were making such a fuss. France, for example, had far more serious bombings during the Algerian crisis. Really good bombings are commonplace in the United States. They come in all styles, there, Britain has a very proper sang-froid about bombings, and a lot of the antics of the Irish nationalists both in Eire and in England are scarcely even noticed by the papers. Here in Canada we would get hysterical.

One of the marks of political maturity is the ability to sneer at the problems of internal nationalism while at the same time coping with them quietly, more or less. On that basis I suppose we Canadians are not politically mature.